VESTIGES_03

Mimesis

reflection as an image of loss

BLACK SUN LIT

VESTIGES_03: Mimesis
reflection as an image of loss

BLACK SUN LIT is the publisher of VESTIGES, an irregularly printed journal of prose, verse, essay, and art that envelops a specific idea or theme unique to each volume.

Single issue: $12.00 U.S.; $16.50 International
Retailers and institutions: Contact Jared D. Fagen, Editor, for discount pricing.

Submissions may be directed to www.blacksunlit.submittable.com. Please read the submission guidelines and open reading periods before sending work.

Queries: editors@blacksunlit.com

www.blacksunlit.com
www.blacksunlit.tumblr.com
www.facebook.com/blacksunlit
@BlackSunLit

Cover illustration: *Affine 1* by Rebecca Norton

ISSN: 2471-7312
ISBN: 978-0-9994312-0-7

Printed in the United States of America

CONTENTS

ACKNOWLEDGEMENTS

BLACK SUN LIT would like to extend special thanks to Erin Fleming, *BOMB Magazine* and the Brooklyn Public Library, Bushel Collective, Ellipsis Press, Contra Mundum Press, Calamari Archive, Unnameable Books, and our digital contributors.

INTRODUCTION TO *MIMESIS*

For Aristotle, art was the faithful imitation of nature, in which beauty could be realized. For Wilde, life was an imitation of art, which operated like a veil and no longer a mirror. Though diametrically opposed in appearance, both claims have in common a consequence of art and perception of reality—that the world is felt as an imperfection, and art an impossibility. Since the Symbolists, art and lived experience have become homogenous in their shared conditions of perpetual transformation and, thus, deception. "We possess of reality," writes Ortega y Gasset, "nothing but the ideas we have succeeded in forming about it." Put another way, existence is also what we dismantle from it; what we embellish or neglect when presenting ourselves to others.

This issue of *Vestiges* explores Plato's truth thrice removed, Pater's sense of facts and Kermode's sense of an ending: words that deal in lies just as the world contracts ideals, expressions made inherently false by that which they attempt to falsify, narratives that reclaim literature from the diegetic, and the artistic rendering of images that are not.

Through this emphasis on the mimetic process and residual loss, contained herein are creative treatments of omission rather than participation; the unattainable instead of the absolute; the visibility of depth and the corruption of surface; the prominence of style and its aberration of the actual; the paratactic in place of progression; and the procedure of thought, not its end result.

EDITOR'S NOTE

Jared Daniel Fagen

Art is not an imitation of nature but its metaphysical supplement,
raised up beside it in order to overcome it.

—Nietzsche

An imitation, more imitation, imitation succeed imitations.

—Gertrude Stein

A lie is the suggestion of a truth. Even truth, historically unreliable, is inherently made counterfeit—a misrepresentation—by its insistence and, more so removed, by our reliance, rehearsal, and inheritance of it. That is truth spent; beaten to death. De Saussure, Jakobson, and Baudrillard suggested (and insisted) this fact in linguistics. As did, of course, Benjamin in art and its aesthetic aura.

Art is a suggestion of life that resembles death by its traces. The semblance is many things: among them an indication, a tinge, or an image culled by an unlikely or stray association with a seemingly disparate object that gains, autonomously, attachment for reasons the image provides no evidence. Art, in this regard, must be something implied but never proven. Art is the wake of fact—the memorial awakens art—in which the consideration of truth becomes the fixed attention toward its immediate dismissal, the uncertainty of life felt by truth's absence.

Reflect upon the frond and in so doing neglect the fern. Write its veins, the stains, its gloss; ponder with inaccuracy its divisive parts. Writing is autumn's discoloration, the experience and expression of wilting. Only stems are left. Imitate and discover what's not there any longer. Reflect if it was ever there at all, or, if it had been, if it was somehow refashioned by the consideration, the treatment, or the way it looked in a certain kind of temper. The writer of loss is a writer that wrests representations into wreckages: a writer trained on a single sun in a star-scattered night, a scrap of litter skimming atop an otherwise undisturbed lake, or a diagonal scar across an antique hope chest, writing their deprivations as fall reduces all to a wither.

A loss of fact (once supported by truth) looks a lot like a loss of meaning. Once in my reflection I found something hideous, but now in this abhorrence is something quite startling. My reflection no longer belongs to a frame but to a tint and tear of light, a likeness half shadowed. Meaning becomes the part of me missing.

November 2017
Brooklyn/Arkville, New York

DID THE MUTE LOSE SOMETHING?

Andrei Codrescu

Monkeys have feelings, people have feelings.
Are people-feelings stronger than monkey-feelings?
Elephants have feelings but they also have memories
longer than either those of monkeys or people.
Monkeys do not have elaborate ceremonies for loss:
it is for them mostly an inner journey of grief, a long trip
the details and intensity of which we cannot understand.
Elephants grieve more elaborately and possibly recall
more accurately every detail from the life of their dead
than the dead might recall themselves if called upon
when still alive. The memory of elephants is divided
between total recall of the lost and symbolic recall
of how one acts (mimes) the loss of a fellow elephant.
Elephants may in fact be more mnemonic than mimetic,
in which case we don't need to talk about them:
they will remember *us*. Monkeys are mimetic to a T.
They are born clowns, imitators of all gestures:
their miming is in fact a pre-mourning for expected loss.
They avant-mourn the loss of themselves. This is why
we will never understand their grieving rituals.
Nor will they understand ours, for the very same reason.
Mimesis for monkeys and people is an art for bypassing
the real, the material, and the density words hopelessly intimate.
We mourn the passing of the reality we mime, imitate, parody
but can only approximate or describe clumsily. Monkeys
leap from tree to tree, choreography by Balanchine, score by Satie.
Us people do it in many words, in styles from Gregorian chant
to laments by Theodor Dreiser or epics by Maxim Gorky.

The elegiac tone of most acceptable poetry is all pre-mourning.
Realism in art and letters is grieving: reality itself grieves
the loss of forms in these works, even the loss of their own
forms of grieving to the assaults of futurism and utopias.
The continual coming and leaving from what we call real
in the mirror of language and the ideograms of poetry consoles.
Whoever stays is grieving as the Chinese poet says: "You go, I stay."
Whoever is leaving no longer grieves until a form of still-life seizes
the absence. Then Loss comes to life to grieve after an image of itself.
What the aggrieved and the departing do is to bemoan the forms
they grew attached to long enough to grieve them, but not as
poignantly as the losers. The left-behind and the gone-ahead
dance a circular grief until their speciae is exhausted.
We call this dance reality or art. The forms of Art are
language and pictures. The purpose of mimesis in art
is to generate forms to set in the vacated space.
These forms have over time become cults of death and genres.
Religions parallel literary genres. Novels are pyramids
in size, Egyptian in scope, parallel to the rise of the desert monogods
that join them later. Poetry is the singular epitaph and can be either
genre or religion: a messenger between forms of grieving
that carries in its claws the Missing and the Lost, epic like the Odyssey
or spare like a tweet. Poets prefer the minimal symbolic remembrance
to better follow the abandon of the "wake" that celebrates forgetting
for an awakening into the life we haven't yet lost.
Grief carried by poetry to the aggrieved is the opposite of loss.
To die is to be lost to the tribe so that the tribe might exult
in songs that are grand, exaggerated, imaginary, abstracted.
Our simple wisdom is that all Loss is abstract,
even if rituals demand a mimesis that is always the same:
an excess of incense and lamentation that is called religion
or an orgy of anamnesis that is verse with or without rhyme.
The novels and essays of death are a stairway to poetry.
We climb it continually, monkeys lending the brevity of living
great effort until we reach the poetry that articulates the gravity

that all live beings instinctively reject.
The construction of death rituals once required shrines, monuments,
churches, robes, mitres, towers and slavery,
but poetry, which requires only climbing into forgetting Loss
by using scant symbols of holding onto the tail of the already-sunk,
can spontaneously and simultaneously grieve and celebrate.
And is quite a bit cheaper, to be frank. It is the angel with the plow.
In the devils' dance of poetry Loss has only an occasional use for Mimesis.
Loss is poetry's reach to living in the present joy of the extra room.
Even photography, pretend queen of mimesis, is only pixels now.

critical addendum

The rituals of genre are those of religion.
Efforts to hybridize genres correspond with the spread of pantheism.
The memoir is not cathartic:
it barely mimes loss with literature and acting.
Religions are forms that invest everything in loss.
Their stories are also the history of literature.
Loss is regret for the failure to riposte
to some quick bon-mot uttered by the lost when they still lived.
Grieving is the mimetic means of merging us with the lost.
Grief can sometimes bring us together with the lost completely, pulling
us to the other side to meet them, thus doubling the loss
for those unwilling to join a collective auto-da-fe.
Others, staggered by such double losses, become greater actors.
In some communities the loss of a husband or a chief is palliated
by the destruction of herm intimates and herm best loved objects.
The wives are burnt alive to mix their ashes with those of their owner.
The domestic vessels are broken, the decorations wrapped
in black linen. In the romantic era post-Werther some lovers died
from reading. They were the suicides of literacy, victims of successful mimesis.
There is alas no longer a surplus of serfs or of romantics,
but the destruction of a lost one's objects is good for capitalism.

Capitalists don't waste more time than necessary worshipping relics.
Apple is coming up with new models, so the last model should be buried
with the lost. Not a big leap, really, since Apple is already
internalized in the lost (but is not a total loss even if disconnected
from its tentacular info sources that are, in this case,
literary and religious). Bury the dead with their tech brands
on the outside so that the visitors of their graves and urns can plug in
and view and hear them from start to finish or at random.
(For heirs only: make sure their last word is their --------.
Mimesis is a skeumorph. The iPhone 9, for example
(August 9, 2017), mimes the 8, but by the time this is published
there is an iPhone X, an eyelash-chip woven
in your eyelashes: you blink to ask Siri what you think.
Compared to the 9 the X is mimetic in the genetic sense:
it shares DNA with the 9 the way we share DNA with monkeys.
Mimesis is symbolic and practiced only as an expression of regret
for the loss of one's own sense of regret, for the duty of mourning
(or) the inability to write, plug in, or charge.
Mimesis is always the Present mourning Loss,
which is always the Past. Moreover the Past
where Loss lives can only be mourned by the Present symbolically,
that is to say through Art. Poetry and all the adjacent genres are
the Mabou Mimes performing Loss using animal instruments.

imitating the dead

existing practices:

1. *Writing/art:* essays, novels, poetry, music whether authored
    or found. Repositories of these forms extant all over the earth in
    libraries, museums, hidden sites, memorized, remembered, buried,
    vanished, reposed in abandoned silos, coded in lost languages.

2. *Methods of disposal:* dividing Loss between members of a family

or tribe to distribute affective specifics; dividing remnants through wills, pillage, theft, or imaginative cons; handing mimetic copies of the literary/art rendition to passersby; stapling to telephone posts, fences, tweeting, posting or describing your Loss to strangers in ways that will move them to think that your Loss is also theirs; reincarnating or re-embodying Loss or the Lost in familiar objects to create Totems; shrinking the oversized qualities of Loss or the Lost (magnified by their disappearance) into tiny objects (beads, tears, raindrops) to continue existence in miniature (like shrunken heads or rice grain paintings); playing Tag with Loss or the Lost by giving *it* to anyone touched by the loser (for example: lightly touching the thin triangle of bare flesh sticking out of an adorably flower-shirt-covered arm whose fingers are clutching a post in the subway car. Or whatever is sufficient for a touched anybody to become *it*); mythologizing Loss and Lost so that it is unrecognizable (like a disguised doll); becoming the Lost and the Loss to cause all concerned to experience *you as it.*

3. Methods of dissemination: mass media; social networks; animated bands; calligraphy; rumors; whispers; hints; unfinished sentences; symbolism; abstractions; random sounds; placing the Lost on heads of statues, passing camels and elephants with oxpeckers and cattle egrets; sneaking *it* into display windows; losing *it* (Loss and the Lost) in public restrooms, garages, cafes, ticket booths, movie and theater seats, on the street, in the woods, in water.

4. Methods of coercion: repeating the same stories about *it* ad nauseam; schools; armies; jails; taking names; mass meetings; social glass houses; demonstrations (planned or spontaneous); oaths of office; inserting *it* in oaths (obscene or ritualistic); attaching *it* (Loss and the Lost) to microchips, dust motes, sand grains, rice grains, microbes, viruses, and yet-unknown means of distribution and recall so as to become contractual (symbiotic) standards.

5. Mimetic avant-guardes: avant-gardes are by definition laments for

Loss and the Lost before they are lost; by miming Loss before it occurs, avant-guardes are making big bets on all other means of remembering, ritualizing, artifacting; pre-mourning precludes the actual mode in which post-Loss activities will occur. That said, post-Loss activities may conform to the forms of pre-Loss because, quite simply, the people of the future are lazy, and the farther in the future we imagine them, the lazier they get.

6.   *Playing dead:* this is easy since only intimates of the Lost or Loss flutter and agitate; the rest, however connected, are playing dead.

7.   *Monumentalism:* this is a process of distortion conducted through the magnification of Loss and the Lost from a family problem to a tribal problem, from a tribal problem to a national problem, from a national problem to a global problem, from a global problem to a cosmic concern; this process is dependent on power: the more power the bigger the ability to project. For an example that can be easily studied: Dag Hammersjköld.

8.   *Erasure:* forget the whole thing. Or see what partial affect will rise from what isn't erased.

9.   *Metamorphoses:* these are the physical and poetic trompe l'oeils that beset or delight the neurotic and may or may not be temporary.

10. *Revenants:* vampires, ghosts, movies, unfashionable hairdos, tacky eras, cultural products stamped zeitgeists, unwelcome ghosts who forgot something in your bed or in your head; the phenomenal world afflicted by insatiability.

11. *Not-yet existing practices so old they can be passed off as brand-new:* reordering angelic hierarchies; status-quoing imagination-based reality; denying loss that isn't in vogue; substituting memory chips (didn't we already list this?); standing in orderly soul-lines to enter new wombs; standing in line to get blowjobs; allowing dreams to

recover parts of Loss; allowing the Lost to be found in imagination or reality only to disappoint by being penetrable and hazy; convincing all parties that the parties they attended never occurred; Loss of the idea of loss through miming amnesia; garter-and-chastity belting: the unborn.

ART SHOW

Greg Mulcahy

Ice gave way and the shanties were gone. Sunk maybe or maybe night stolen.

The trio, Nesto and Goat Cheese and Water Snake, going about claiming to be artists.

Some late portrait.

The three as artifacts found in a motel room.

Modern picture for room or lobby—whole firms that made them.

Not these three.

Arrived via transfer and was the boss now again gone?

Picture of nothing but arrangement.

Never make a world that way.

Measure and result. Tap or tapping. Link or hitch.

As though complexity were flexibility.

Wisconsin—some—was in there.

And despair.

This Nesto reproduced children's toys and knick-knacks in shiny materials and sold them for fortunes to idiot companies and municipalities. Goat Cheese and Water Snake either promoters or toadies in tow.

Big Wife had tossed Nesto years ago.

Nesto claimed the toss made his career.

It was dreams of the machine, Goat Cheese said.

We're but slaves to the future, Water Snake agreed.

Big Wife vowed she'd serve Nesto crumbs in vinegar. If that.

Before Big Wife, Nesto called a piece.

Some thing about a golden ballerina.

As though Nesto had a dancer ever met.

Nesto insisted all Nesto had ever wanted was a community of understanding.

It was not, Nesto insisted, that Nesto had been or sought the suitor weird.

Big Wife might not agree.

Nesto claimed to have made such art as laid the Jesus joke upon us, but when pressed for the work, said it among the lost.

Bark, bark, bark, bark, someone said.

It might have been Goat Cheese who often seemed to play a proscribed role.

Or Water Snake who asserted he had once seen a great ape drinking at a well of whiskey.

No one believed that.

Commonly understood as a bit of atmospherics in preparation of some larger spectacle.

Nesto did not look like someone who ran an artistic trio.

Everyone who saw Nesto saw clearly Nesto had been something else before Nesto involved himself in the art world, and it was equally obvious Nesto had likely not been known as Nesto long.

Goat Cheese faced no such scrutiny, for Goat Cheese scarcely registered.

Water Snake as slithered as his sobriquet, driving their battered vehicle about, signed with promise of some coming show in pathetic publicity attempt.

Show constantly rescheduled. Rescheduled so often no one any longer listened to the explanations for delay.

How or where this show was to occur never clearly specified. Instead, mere mutter of potential venues.

Part of the problem with the show Nesto asserted involved the complicated question of curation, which was not merely a question but really more an investigation of the notion of curation.

No one was much aroused by these assertions.

Water Snake claimed to have studied curation with the great master at the capital but insisted out here in the provinces there was nothing like the resources available to one in the capital.

Goat Cheese took an opposite position insisting his experience was only that of a working artist who left the curation to others, curation being a discipline unto itself as foreign from working art as Chinese was from Russia.

Nesto suggested the three might put on a panel for the instruction of the populace.

This proposal tavern made.

There could be, Nesto suggested, sample of the art he and his comrades claimed to have created, though those who had seen the samples said the samples looked machine-made.

Art, Nesto said, was by definition manufactured.

No one asked what Nesto meant by manufactured.

Goat Cheese gave a long speech that seemed to be about the necessity or the necessary.

No one suggested it had anything to do with pictures.

Some one asked who this trinity thought its audience was and Water Snake recited a proclamation from an extinct movement.

No one had heard of it.

Then Nesto was on about some chronicle or another.

Maybe it was a tale.

Nesto produced some samples, but the samples were slides of what Nesto claimed were paintings, but there was no projector, so anyone who wanted to look had to hold a slide to light source and look.

The slides looked like splotches of primary colors muddily intermingled.

This for what, Nesto said.

This is to what end, Nesto said.

Nesto went on to declare the splotches were scientifically aligned to produce specialized, predictable effect based upon a series of proprietary formulas.

Water Snake said until Water Snake had found science Water Snake had wandered lost in Water Snake's own life.

Goat Cheese said the formulas were formulated precisely with Inner Peace in mind.

And, Water Snake added, on view.

Nesto claimed to have put on a big show at the Theater of Two Brothers. The show was supposedly called *Beautiful, Happy Place*. Water Snake said the show had been called *1,000 Pieces of Silver*. Nesto said Water Snake was confused because Water Snake had a long history of confusion and was fortunate, in his confusion, to have Nesto to help him, to offer him aid, to bring him about from place to place, to consult with him on his work, to arrange for him the necessary arrangements, and all of this, and so much more, without a thought of compensation or of Nesto's well being, or of Nesto's necessity of contemplation, or of Nesto's profound mission, nor of Nesto's essential work.

This, Nesto said, was clarity clearly applied.

Nesto ever on about the plastic nature of the objects that were to populate the show, if the show were to occur.

Water Snake no longer mentioned it.

Goat Cheese seemed increasingly indifferent as Goat Cheese roamed the area in brightly colored costume.

A costume, Nesto said, designed by Nesto for an earlier show, but when Nesto was pressed, Nesto insisted that earlier show was a show of an entirely different kind than the show Nesto was currently planning. The earlier show, Nesto said, had not demanded any curation from Nesto while the planned show, obviously, demanded all of Nesto's power to curate, which was, really, nothing but a prolonged act of concentration in action.

When Goat Cheese's picture was described by Water Snake as a splotch, Goat Cheese responded, Exactly so, as in life.

Water Snake asked if it was symbolic.

As a leader is symbolic, Goat Cheese said, framed as though in leaderly narration.

The symbolic leadership, Water Snake said, more symbol than technocrat as the splotch indicates.

It is indicative, Goat Cheese said. I am pleased that you have attained this level of appreciation.

Perhaps, Water Snake said, it is in anticipation of some reciprocity.

What in our activities would or should not be, Goat Cheese said, pointing to the splotch.

Nesto insisted the splotch was a circle although the circle was not circular.

Would you prefer, Nesto said, it was referred to as a line?

That was a discussion for the catalog, Water Snake said. To have the discussion now, at this stage in planning the show, was premature. When the catalog writer was selected, that was the time to discuss the entries or potential entries for the catalog.

Nesto became enraged.

I will not, Nesto said, engage in another catalog argument. A catalog argument has torpedoed many a show.

That was not what happened in the other place, Goat Cheese said.

The other place, Nesto said, is another place. This place is not that place. This experience is not that experience. There is no comparison. None. And none tolerated.

We've got an original coming, Nesto said. A discovery. Valuable and valued, yes, but not for me to value it. My role is to protect and nourish it.

Water Snake drank something from a flask. Goat Cheese nudged Water Snake, and Water Snake handed him the flask.

I heard, Water Snake said, it was *The Salvation*.

We'll watch something die, Goat Cheese said, when we sell that novelty.

Commerce is not my domain, Nesto said. I dwell in the realm of aesthetics.

Always death of something, Goat Cheese said.

And the fantastic rendering, Water Snake said, we'll genuflect to it or resist. Makes no difference.

You'll genuflect to role or title superior, Nesto said. As you always have. And will.

Aren't we really, Goat Cheese said, disputing the divided Heart of Something and not the question of the sacred?

Don't ask inquest grim, Nesto said. Sacred leads only to the hostile heart of definition.

Definition, Water Snake said, it's no secret message. Little secret or individual about it.

Now, Nesto said, you see? You're bringing Snake to dogma when we want to focus on exhibition. Or are you after a goodbye instead of all?

It's a poor exhibition if you're the only one in it, Goat Cheese said.

And what, Nesto said, would you be captioned—Dog, Ape, or Ass?

If something is sacred, Water Snake said, it is a factual matter. A factual matter is by definition a matter beyond dispute. All this is well established.

We have not yet formed, Nesto said, a debating society, but I understand your conflict, and clearly it's borne of lack of concrete detail. Yet well you know it is too early to reveal much. But we might suppose. Suppose for example we had dog-headed piece from Egyptian or Persian era and some feature of petrified bread and broken arrow. Sound a bit like a bit of something we might know. Sharpen a dagger on that one.

Luxury, Water Snake said.

This is not, I hope, Goat Cheese said, part of the battle to reinstate the imagined past.

A tower rose, Nesto said. Towers fall. Plenty of depictions of falling towers.

Plenty of representations, Goat Cheese said, of Mound of Turf.

And that, Nesto said, should be the totality of ambition? Forget art, beauty, truth, nobility and instead embrace a pile of mud. I sometimes wonder why we are associated. What is our goal here but to bring the finer things to this community? And for this I am paid in futility as my associates not only resist me, not only quarrel, but seem hell bent on building, not the finest exhibition we can, but instead some accident. As beauty becomes truth, so does decline become collapse. Or is that what you are after?

Oh Roger, Goat Cheese said, she worked me then.

It was the discipline, Water Snake said, or it was the indiscipline—one did it.

Isn't that, Goat Cheese said, the bloated corpse of the thing in a nutshell?

Old clam hand, Water Snake said, when it's time to settle up the tavern.

Does either of you recall, Nesto said, whatever became of Baldo McLarden?

McLarden, Water Snake said, was found all afloat.

With a bullet in his head, Goat Cheese said, and all that never solved.

Not solved, Nesto said, nor even puzzled. Tell me, had either of you business with Baldo?

No, Water Snake said, I'd not deal with that crook.

Neither me, Goat Cheese said. Money vanished when Baldo was about.

Yet, Nesto said, neither of you did anything about it. Or as much about it as the ape without a mirror stood naked before his notebook.

I've told you, Water Snake said, there never was a notebook.

Noted, Nesto said.

Or not, Goat Cheese said.

You sit around, Nesto said, screaming BAMBOO SALAD CLAWS all day, but that does not make for prophecy.

And what has that to do, Water Snake said, with Baldo's final end?

If I weren't an artist, Nesto said, I'd draw you a picture. However my work is too valuable for that.

Is there no bottom to this fall, Goat Cheese said.

How about a visit, Nesto said, to the Humiliation Department? Perhaps that's the correction you seek.

And you, Goat Cheese said, I hear there's a sign Failure to Adequately Progress beneath your picture.

Why don't we end this ceaseless quarrel, Water Snake said. It was amusing for awhile, but in the end, it brings us nothing.

In the end, Goat Cheese said, there is nothing.

You know what a down boat is, Nesto said.

Put it in the all painted wall, Water Snake said. You think you offer manifestation which can not be understood. Many the hack has or is hidden there.

If a dog, Nesto said, started outside the clown tent, who deserted the circus, or the circus deserted whom?

What happened, Goat Cheese said, to our project cartography of paradise? What green book gave that life?

Another clever joke exchange, Nesto said. Have you two nothing more than that? Must I regret whatever Trampville I rescued you from? And for that—is this gratitude?

Exchanged to death, Water Snake said.

Let die of neglect, Goat Cheese said.

Idiot, Bastard, Nesto said. Traitors!

Fish a come, Water Snake said. Fish a kill.

Come back, Goat Cheese said. Come back to kill near or a' the sea there.

Fish, Nesto said. I was never in the fish business. I don't care what you say. I don't care what you heard. Or where. I know I have enemies aplenty. But I had nothing to do with fish, or fishing, or fish products. I have never been to the city of Duluth, much less Superior. This has been well documented. It is all in the records. And guess what—there is no record of my having visited those places. There could not be because I have never done it. Oh, I know false charges. Sometimes I think I know false charges better than anything else.

Is he, Goat Cheese said.

Almost, Water Snake said.

Soon, Goat Cheese said.

In a minute, Water Snake said. Let the fish build in him. That will bring it on. Look at him. It's as though a fish had swallowed him. He cannot let go of it. It surrounds him and blinds him. He is contained inside it. Imprisoned, you might say.

I was never, Nesto said, charged nor imprisoned. I have never spent a night in jail, much less prison. Not in any jail. Not in this country or in any other country, state, or municipality. Again, all this has been looked at. I am not in the records. I could not be.

NESTO'S SPEECH

The whale is the sign of the Leviathan as our literature insists and must insist. This Leviathan will be, as it has been in the past, loosed. Love no more than is necessary, for what is loved shall be destroyed. HA HA HA HA HA HA. Tell the funny joke again and again while you are still able. Your painted faction feels no loyalty. It is indifferent to this desire. Do not expect a carefully managed breakdown. If you see it coming, will you see it fall? Coming is falling. Seeing is falling. Sooner, later, every one. The source of afterwards known only in afterwards. That is when you know. Afterwards. Until then you cannot know because you will not know. Your corruption will condemn you to that truth you are condemned to anyway—that truth beyond escape—that truth that relentlessly pursues and will be satisfied only when it declares itself satisfied. All this long prophesied in the prophecy. The human margin, what you know of it, and it, really, is all you know, is locked in, and a lock can only be opened—this lock—with the inevitable key. There is no escape from ultimate reality and evasion will be temporary at best. Faced with reality, there will be distortion of personality followed by disappearance of personality. You will be left with nothing. Nothing you destined and though it is beyond your understanding, your destiny. Do not mistake destiny for reward. Ask yourself what have you done to deserve reward. Ask and await the answer come as judgment deserved, as action not word, as form, form the realization of being. Come to that when it comes to you and no plea nor prayer shall stop it, or delay it, or alter it. Then the reality of your destruction and the futility of your resistance shall finally triumph in the face of your arrogance, your cowardice, your weakness, your falsehood. You will see yourself for the weak nothing you are—as loss—as absence, as shadow without flesh in the unfleshing. And what will remain? All your cringing appetite that you imagined justified substance. Where will your pompous greed be when the cheap costume of agency is stripped away and the naked self-service you mistake as assertion historic and heroic is no more. You can beg. You will beg. But beggar, let me tell you this—expect a beggar's dinner at best. At best, what kindly mercy do you expect to find you? You are too blind to see. You are too deaf to hear. You are too stupid to understand. Yet none of this is known to you. Signs surround you, but you cannot recognize a sign, any sign at all. In your luxuriant idiocy you luxuriate and take it for correct action, yet who, have you ever asked yourself, does the action serve? You and only your yapping maw of appetite endless and base. You roll in your own filth like a cur in a rich man's yard unaware of what true treasure is, much less where it might be found. You yelp like a cur at your dumb pleasure and blinder pain. If you cannot see this in the clear of day, you know it unseen or seen in the dream of night. It is not a matter of revelation but of what has been long revealed and continues to be revealed. Darkness will descend as darkness always descends as in the brightest light you remain in the dark and in that dark shall every creature come and dwell therein as all this began long ago, before imagination, before formed concept. Time will collapse having served the purpose time must serve and, after purpose, superfluous. All that is not necessary will fall away and the hunter may hunt or think to hunt, but the hunter will fear the blood, and comes another hunter, fearless, that fearless hunter begun as death.

Nesto stopped talking.

Goat Cheese and Water Snake fell on Nesto. They beat him, knocked him to the ground, kicked and stomped him, pummeled Nesto until Nesto stopped moving.

Is he out, Goat Cheese said.

He's out, Water Snake said. Went out faster this time.

Just as well. Who has the energy anymore for a long beating? Remember that time out West?

Yeah. It took a lot of beating to drive out those demons. He's either got weaker demons or he's faster on the re-set.

So much the better, Goat Cheese said. Once he is no longer possessed, we can continue with the project. One sees these events depicted so frequently in the classical works.

Nesto sputtered.

I taste weak sencha, Nesto said.

How's the memory, Water Snake said.

Of what? Nesto said.

That's right, Goat Cheese said. That's just fine.

A masterpiece, Nesto said, of beauty, we were going to have. Is that it? Something about footprints in the sand and the savior?

That's close enough, Water Snake said. We're on a project.

When aren't we, Nesto said. It's one the next. I don't know where I anymore get the energy.

After this, Goat Cheese said, we'll take a long rest. God knows we've earned it.

God, Nesto said.

It's an expression, Water Snake said.

Yeah, Nesto said. Sure.

A crudely-rendered messiah, Water Snake said, filling us with remorse.

Penance, Nesto said, is demanded.

And remorse, Goat Cheese said. There is really no other way.

It is a way, Nesto said, of finding the reduction in everyone.

Needs some underwriting, Water Snake said. You know, community support.

Our project could use that, Nesto said. Something that tells people they are who they want to be. Drive that home.

We'll never, Water Snake said, construct that.

Why, Nesto said, what else? What other possibility.

It is not about possibility, Goat Cheese said. Or sustainability. We are after the exhibit of object.

As saint, Nesto said, or relic. Statue or picture. Rag, even. Who cares what as what? It is all a matter of when.

When it's possible, Water Snake said, why should it not be equally sustainable.

This one, Goat Cheese said, does not understand event.

We'll need, Nesto said, twenty pages of notes a day for the catalog alone. How do we generate that?

Get, Water Snake said, some professor to do it for free.

Knew a professor, Goat Cheese said, sold soap or something door-to-door. Long time ago. Things were different then.

Now, Nesto said, we're here. That is always true. Until—you know what I mean.

In that long, black night, Water Snake said, without moon or stars.

Enough, Goat Cheese said.

Enough, Nesto said.

Enough, Water Snake said.

No more, Nesto said. More would kill the whole thing. We keep it alive as long as we can.

We cannot, Goat Cheese said, yield to confusion of motive.

To do so, Water Snake said, would lead us inevitably to confusion of action.

Was that a problem, Nesto said.

The question of problem, Goat Cheese said, is not the question under examination.

The problem does not matter, Water Snake said.

Formed a cross, Nesto said, what did—that scar—what else—vehicles in the crash—so that tells you—is there a picture.

Nothing, Water Snake said, torn from binding cheap.

Easier, Goat Cheese said, to envision a field populated of God's creation.

And how, Nesto said, do we find our way out of here?

This has to also, Water Snake said, be about connection.

Solidarity, Nesto said, is hard to come by.

I speak, Water Snake said, more fiscally than spiritually.

Nothing wrong with that, Goat Cheese said.

We've got to eat, Nesto said.

And more, Goat Cheese said.

Maybe, Water Snake said, you never been in a tanked operation.

Sold water tanks once, Nesto said, out in some drought country.

What country isn't, Water Snake said.

Question, Goat Cheese said, of immediacy then.

Then, Nesto said.

There, Goat Cheese said. Where we were.

Where was that, Nesto said.

Who remembers, Water Snake said.

Why anybody would, Goat Cheese said, has always been beyond me.

Sometimes, Nesto said, I think art was a poor choice.

An option, Water Snake said, is an option.

Don't be, Goat Cheese said, a victim of wasting consciousness.

Can one not, Water Snake said, seek the perfection of artifice?

You're shooting too high, Nesto said.

And you, Goat Cheese said.

Got to take a delivery, Nesto said.

Crated, Water Snake said.

What else, Nesto said.

What fearful desire, Goat Cheese said, will be more or less displaced in the discovery of this delivery?

Displaced? Water Snake said. Replaced, I should hope.

Hope, Nesto said.

And some drama enact, Water Snake said.

Well, one or the other, Goat Cheese said.

Which to which, Nesto said. However to whatever.

Lest my heart betray me, Water Snake said.

If you have one, Goat Cheese said.

It always will, Nesto said. Always.

Or something, Goat Cheese said.

When do we finish this, Water Snake said.

And, Nesto said.

Leave, Water Snake said.

Leave to what, Goat Cheese said.

To the next thing, Water Snake said. The thing after, you know.

And some day, Nesto said, to write all this out in tome massive to record for posterity.

And a film, Water Snake said, made of it all, and all of us therein depicted.

Depicted, Goat Cheese said. I'd play myself and how ever else not?

Path fraught with stumbles, Water Snake said.

Stumbles and risks, Nesto said.

Risks and rewards, Goat Cheese said.

What do you want me to do? Nesto said. You want me to call, Hey There Patty Sausage?

Come to the picture, Water Snake said.

This crate, Goat Cheese said, is empty. This is not our treasure.

Not, Nesto said, what we planned. True. For what did we want but something to reveal, at last, a treasure, and come to end in peace, in love, in beauty?

FIVE POEMS

Lindsay Remee Ahl

In the Land of "Let Me Roll It To You"

In the history of physics, it was clear by 1907 that the atom
      was substantially empty space.

I call my teenage son, who is in New York. "I've been playing Lake
Street Dive's
      cover, *Let Me Roll It,* since you're not here," I tell him.

"*Someone's* got to," he says.
      Every morning, he used to play *Let Me Roll It* and *I Don't Mind*

by James Brown, live at the Apollo in 1962, as loud
      as his speakers could take the sound.

This morning, I woke to the absence of his music, my dreaming
      substantially empty space.

I had been wondering fiercely about the voice within—how
      to follow it at all costs no matter where it takes me?

In the wake of empty space, I walk streets through morning light,
      end up in a dry river bed, sand deep, the street merging into river

sand, arroyo past low slung houses, ragged cottonwoods.
      When I look up the street sign says *Griffin Street.*

I lean into a wall, glance over, and there, on someone's mailbox:
        Au Griffon, a little schulpture, like the one beside the doorway

to the Chette Shop in Paris, 1901. My theory on the empty space
        in an atom—that's what the Griffins were supposed to be guarding.

The secrets got by them, each slow discovery added up.
        "I'm in Strand Book Store," my son says, "what Hume
should I buy?"

My encounter with Hume was brief, that military expedition
        to Brittany in 1747, during which he was working on his thoughts

on Events—they are either *caused* or not and sometimes we can figure
out which.
        History begins as empty space, either written or not written,

created or not created, and in that arena the physicists watched
        the atoms in all their spatial glory and too witnessed

the electrons jumping their orbit. According to Hume, the moral evil
allowed
        by God on earth is "beyond reason" and therefore beyond
philosophy.

At the unknown interview in the foyer, Griffins guarding, they were playing
        Let Me Roll It—even though the song wasn't written yet, even
though

my son wasn't born yet. If your son went to war and died for his country.
        If Rutherford disintegrated a nitrogen atom into an oxygen atom

in 1918, and by 1932 had accessed forces not mechanical, by splitting an
atom.
        We used to ask, "Are you worthy of the music you listen to?"

a challenge we welcomed, the answer usually "no," as music opens questions

of *sublime mystery* akin to Hume explaining the snake in the garden.

Really, *What isn't beyond reason?* in the end.

In Answer To The Question

I once saw several horses dawning white
at dawn and I once saw

the terrace of the lions, time receding
so quickly heaven and earth were joined

together at the altar in the corner of the city park
sunlight cathexis

it had been holy

all of it, sacred

every time
I looked at you

all of time, all arrived

as an *auto-de-fé*—an *act of faith*
to be burned at the stake
to give yourself to love

Invisibles

Alone with the shaft of light
      from the hallway, smoky
haze of cigarette smoke
      as figures walk by, the voice
of Walter Cronkite in the background.

Alone and invisible, a clear visage walking
      through walls.

      say: illusion
      say: body and blood
      say: born of a woman
      say: you see me

        but did I ever argue to be seen?

Alone with moontime, luna, selene, lua, lune,
      mirror of all peoples,
mirror of light,
      turn around and fight for your life.

Night Tone

I parachute in
memorize the map

descend the garden path
in the dancing shadows of the willow

infiltrate

the old military base still live with mines
trees growing out of the interstate

> what seemed solid, the brick building we lived in,
> the street corner I waited on to hold my child's hand—
> vanished in a breath

night all around, rain falling, I hear a crack—
a tree plummets to the road right before me

but I'm still standing as though
all of space-time is exquisitely

balanced
between existing or not

The Last Thing

If this is the last thing
you write?

What world?

Only a feeling,
not language.

A bowing down.

IN WHICH SHE IS UNBUTTONED BY ABSENCE & HE IS HIS OWN APARTMENT BUILDING

Erin Slaughter

I

vulnerable began to feel / like a kind of light / but was probably only mirror-stuff / like so much

of what she found herself / clawing out of her own skin for / she is afraid of heights / & abandonment / & every noun in the corner of her eye / is a wolf /

disembodied city / empty / stomach digests itself / emptiness she cradles / like a proud parent / she tells him that she trusts him because she trusts him / but what choice does she have / when she continues / to let him unstitch her / grope around for something

like a clock / she trusts him / to knit her into something that could pass / for *person* / shivers when she lies / back on the carpet / & he watches her with nothing resembling need

II

fantasy is a slower violence / that infiltrates the body / *I open into a wound for you & you won't even make me bleed* / how will this ever be clean / without a burning? / she has a sad dumb loyalty to

every lost life / she's lived / more of a surgery each time to pry away /

morsels of skin & hair & whatever / fold-out love she's decided / to call home / her emptiness

unbuttoned by absence / wasted in rooms / unoccupied / wasted pola-roids / on the sliver of lamp perching her nose / she drives at night

& sitting beside him thinks *we will starve here feasting / adulation on each other but why?* / sad dumb loyalty

III

descends into wildness madness / promises / she will be brave for this / it always comes down to the gnawing / hollow gnawing / a haunting / named *I want to go home but I am home I want / to go home but home is walking away*

in a gray sweater / ascending the stairs & would hate me / if he knew the capacity of my hunger / & he is his own apartment building / rent-controlled inhabit-ed / by a collection of fish-women / anyway he's sleeping / & she's still sitting / in a parked car / so

ideally tomorrow a fresh coat / of makeup a little mania in her coffee / which she hopes tastes like peppermint / come / fearless autumn leaving

EXCERPTS from *GAPS IN THE CHASE*

Adam Greenberg

Most threads drag a little water. The upright body is the exception. With her, suddenly away, body. Worn thin of the shore's scopes and sight. To the hill, overhead, to the tram. To the hill from poor judgment. Judgment not the exit to dead sounds: the merely described men we know. He said to eat a bit more, to follow an "entire white rasping" by following the island's silks, pearls, and crevasses: sun on the rocks. Rocks under the ribs. Hands there to hold it.

A touch might be the hidden touch of quantity. What depth intends. What depth remains nervous, clear life and supposed days, gold away, he says. Anything less is sentimental. The round thick curls of fog, dogs, donors and such. The turn is grinded with "so many others," as the cats along the dock who sit and eat sardines, moths, and excess bones. Beside her neck to the hand in gulping once with pinkish water. Around the back as she opened the window. The "different feeling" as I saw him and I opened the window, she says.

Often something so hungered is as tentative. The moon more than intact seems attached, she says, the thinner example: the side where one and one are visible restores the partial part. A fisherman says it must be the body, must arrest one's body as if slipping, still, catching fish, slipping on moss and mold. To be nevertheless thin, she says. And then climbing the hill? With a hand in hand and wringing along the tram.

For planting hinders rumors. The glance when we dock at the opposite bank. Angle apart that it's worse near the wall, he says. We profess: did we eat as much as we can? Shall we dig a bit deeper? The earth opens to ordinary little. One claims another kindness. The sail was a line through the night, without having been caught, as all good geometry like a dry sea takes its many colors and angles.

All described matters, if for example safe, dead reading, are safe. Invisible matters are said "to be revolving" and "not to complain." At the observatory, she says, through glass we see the stars, always at night, at night from the points of our scopes. The silver bit's the men we know, an ore perhaps, most often a reflection in water. There's something cosmic about it, particularly in my voice. As I've hardly sent for someone I knew.

FOUR POEMS from *HEARTBROKER*

Tony Mancus

1.

Gone tangible and so

this wood splitspelled its name

wrong along the ground it grew from

We'll be folded into it together

Say the word bone and New Years say the word until

it never hits your teeth

A set of streets bark their lights on

Say something trill, loving, monstrous

then the retreat of your mouth, I will help you carry it, heartbroker

Hands like the face of god—chains dipped in oil

one prayer mean in its urgency

on your lips I screen the mutual plane we inhabit but

Don't feel grown—trademarked and capital

I celebrate losses—every friend and lover, their sketches what's the word

Burrowing further now

Missionary and then uncomfortable and then   The yeahs in every
song we shout together

I can only do so much   damage and then stay quit   say it

Only so many flipped wands and numbered cups to sell this future, a
quilt of guesses knit to the same end

Saw how we were meant to stray but like the idea of a dog we're always
something biting at always something limping home, no current dim lit
under our skin, no licking holes. No way up the worn worn-out
mountains. Call them round and top and hill and back to the center
they come crawling.

2.

I am not sick with emotion. It's just, what drowns in me. As a question.

When the chairs are on fire and the memory of a lake settles its choppy water, you can enter the scene like someone from a different history. All the blades dull and drawered. You melt the candle down around the light it spits. Maybe another patch of sky like a bruise. The flat edge raising up to show.

You take the pieces and put them in your mouth when it's evening. I am certain that there's something about leaving a place that makes it difficult to see. We don't know how to bend toward or other ways that could be considered natural. If the sequence of events were round us. I am going to leave this body here for later. You are going to assemble the forest from its echoes. One way to build a haunt. Pick up the left things and ask them to talk.

One parts and replaces. A dream becomes a nuisance after you form your heartstone, after it cracks like an egg against your pursuit. The wall of it. The wailing. The hide thick afterwards. How you cut back to love like a question. Three knives you can shoot. A whole program devoted to this.

Alternatives included. Whisper them to me. How they fork and branch.

Distance makes the heart, they say. Molds it flat and onto your shirt. Clay or stone or magic marker. You pick the person, but not the time. You place the map and find yourself, maybe. I draft the papers up. I ask them to say their sayings back to us. Fan blades move the air.

When it's time to say goodbye. That feeling like a stave. Right through.

3.

Try to place the memory back into its habitation. Absolutes don't fare well through the ages. Worn into the woods, anybody can pry their skin off.

If I swear my sickness has nothing to do. Listen to the space between the words. How a breath draws itself back out without having to dwell too long inside us. What happens to the air that never gets released completely. Baby chirp, the lasting effects of accumulation. Sing this life like it's a keening. What percent gets left behind.

Laying the wares on the table. Little instruments for valves and chambers. The metal in your blood enough to weight it.

Let's circle back to the last stop. I don't remember how to pull this language through the hoop, but you will it so. Happiness dements the receiver. But it's a product like others demand. It can be quantified. Somebody dancing like they're alone in a crowd. The smell after a controlled explosion and people clapping at the dark that turns bright for a moment.

Think of your sandblasted memories. A cut in the wood. An erasure sets too. Similar things in the same place make it hard to judge.

4.

How old is the break you took, what performance/wingthief
kleptomania/a new suit of cards to shower the night with—edges swing
and sway like lovers on a glider, their hands building a language between
them. For each other and back.

Saying something makes it real. Saying nothing makes it quiet. All the
volleys built into space there.

When you say the words you wish would make you fall apart. Pieces of
you like confetti in a charm. In a champagne flute. In the tar and dust.
How to mouth the feeling into being. I cannot inhibit your discernment,
but might be able to watch you rise. I could ask the same question every
morning. Risen. Rinsed. Replete with intonation. Maybe this is feeling
too, fleeting as it is.

A GREAT RIVER

Victor Segalen
translated from French by Jonathan Larson

I know not whence it courses exactly. It itself doesn't know and even less so does the Genie that permeates it, animating and marking all its projections. It's thus that the spirit of the River, – the afterlife of which this leaves no doubt, I hope, – not living and not existing but there where the mighty River has taken on all its conscience, and taken on all its liquid and successive personality. And it's why, having chosen only to honor the Genie of the River by this, I have not delayed myself in deciding, whether if down there, in the full heart of Tibet, whether it's *that* vein of water or else this one, each wholly alike, which truly is its origin. As with an unformed newborn, all the torrents, down there, contain all possibilities : a hundred *li* of what is more, to the east or to the west, and this stream will possibly become the sad and sniveling Houang-ho, half-drunk by the muds of the north, or even the Mekong or the Salween, opening itself to the thousands of days under the tropics, or even, by the most glorious of fortunes, the mighty River itself, the Yangtze-Jiang, puncturing the immense Empire with its willful arcs round as an orange as juicy as this fruit near putrefaction. But despite all of this, even so the spirit of the River doesn't really know it. No more than the number of places it courses through ; no more than the surface area of its basin ; perhaps only the number of tributaries that it doesn't know apart from the struggle of an instant ; and knowing just exactly whether it's the fourth or fifth of the great flows of water matters little to it, in the long run ; the second could be suspended by the density of the earth… For it's in every River's destiny to know no other river apart from itself.

The destiny of all the great rivers nothing apart from being unique in the world, and each one for itself without touching others but to absorb them. The Spirits of the mountains that can contemplate themselves freely are more fraternal from one summit to another, or even to conjoin through the subterranean veins. The River, even this close up, ignores all of its congeners. It doesn't separate itself from the immense subterranean cloth but to course straightaway a fierce singular life, isolated by barriers that its Genie will not surmount, and from there, one knows toward which sea it will dissolve... That the ways would be parallel or not, that the waters would have the same virtue, the two flows would pursue themselves as if they alone existed in the different orbs of the sky... Even its tributaries, it neither receive them nor knows them but to absorb them whole straight-away in itself, with struggles and sometimes violent eddies. Every river is bound to be unique and incomparable. The good life, fierce and haughty, without connection but the long thread of its course.

That there, the Genie of the River senses it obscurely and powerfully. And this Genie doesn't exist apart from the moment where in assembling, the River has affirmed its own power ; at the moment where it exists willfully, as the same, and not otherwise, at the moment where it's at its maximum, it, the Great Flow. That's when it possesses its life, its tumultuousness, its flooding and thinning out, its rages, its repentances, a low-water lapping, tides that guide the stars, and others, peculiarities, that guide neither the sun nor the moon ; its eddies, its leaps, its diva-gations, and also the parasites of its bright skin : the freight junks and the pleasure junks ; the vermin of its banks : the coolies of the towpath, their women, their adventitious villages. It's also at this very moment that it goes through the worst obstacles and with the greatest vigor. It's at this moment that its personality shatters, the chosen moment of its life. It's there that its Genie encloses itself as within the innermost of the human.

*
* *

It's the moment of Rapids and Gorges. For a long time reinforced by the Jialing, then by the Fu river, abounding, solid, up against all the ruses of the mountain, oriented firmly and conscious of its course (it wants to move toward the east ; it finally decided once and for all to throw itself into the oriental sea and not at all into the gulf of the Annam tributary), it will roll from bank to bank, to descend in unfolding, delivering itself to corridors full of clashes... all of this, from Chongqing to Yichang to the heart of the city of Sichuan, center and queen of the eighteen provinces and of the country of Bod, at the center of the orange that it pierces. That's the moment of its great maturity, of its full violence : the Defiling of Rapids and Gorges.

*
*   *

Since before the promontory of Chongqing ; placed there to mark its departure in this new life it already possesses its beautiful, savorous color. It has already ground down many mountains, it has licked many red, ochre, grey or bluish clays that mix and blend all of these dusts, its waters have taken on a particular shimmering. Point of imbecilic transparency, point of naiveté as in the eyes of the sources ; but this opalescence made iridescent, changing ; nothing of glass nor of cold... The long communion of the banks and the water have produced this unctuous course where indiscrete eyes stop and that allows nothing to be seen of its abysses, apart from the changing reflections, rusty and blue, depending on whether it's the liquid body's color or rather the sky's reflection mirrored on its opacity.

It's there at the very bottom where its ungraspable body is elongating the old Genie of an incomprehensible existence, it's there, under the marvelous muds, and each atom, each suspended grain, shocking to the others is a parcel of the memory of the river that can count its detours this way, its contributions, its whirls of yesteryear. It's in rolling through these lands and these myriads that the river remembers itself and continues. The slowly rusted metallic parcels dissolve little by little in the lively waves, communicating their savor and losing their specificity...

And sometimes, from the hollows of the bed, all of a sudden a burst of half-forgotten riffles rises so that one of these movements of peculiar water all of a sudden flush out vertically at its surface. The river remembers itself : this is come from the fragrant Yunnan ; or else, without specifying, it's the forgotten contribution of one of the confluences and the river worries itself over this riffle and this flavor that doesn't come from itself. The Genie of the river twitches as at the approach of a menacing thing by unknown sound.

The promontory of Chongqing is a departure in the life of the adult, – the ardent and powerful life of the river. A riffle at Chongqing marks its enormous shoulders. It's there that the river Jialing comes rushing all of a sudden. At first, a spur separates them ; they will unite when the mountain intervenes brusquely, and here there's a double riffle. The two enemies have diverged brusquely, then return one on top of the other. But all is divergent, all is different amongst themselves : the contents of the waters, and their volume, and the low-water and the level (the one in the full floods of summer perhaps without the other having yet given a sign). And from this discord terrible eddies are borne sometimes. And if they are even and slow, all is smooth. But as soon as the Jialing swells up all of a sudden, here conical whirls form with the regularity of a slow respiration from the right to the left bank. The water, below, turns in circles as in a circus with a recourse to the center, a spiral curl dying in the middle of an implacable effect. It's a mouth moving from the flow, a movable mouth, sucking, full of violent water and agglutinated, by a water that catches and won't let go anymore. That a living prey, of human life, who is temporary and of a different fluvial (mineral, vegetal, animal) reign, were to come and touch the edge, and just as soon be destined to the depths. The river, the cascade, the water, alone, which penetrates all, has obtained this indefinite fluidity, always in movement, always renewed, always the semblance of itself.

Like circular water, it will just as soon make a roundabout. The human parasite feels the danger strongly. One sees it beating hurriedly from every leg of the junk, from every effort of its eight little men, sometimes before, sometimes after, but advancing when it wants to move back and diverting when it wants to advance, always implacably turning in circles. Then it reaches toward the middle, descending accordingly, for the well-formed mouth is hollow, hollow beneath the levels of winter's waters. And then the junk, right in the middle, twirling foolishly around itself. Its head is accounted for, it plunges, the backside in the air, breathing in, wedged, held, drank up whole by the Flow. The large mouth smooths out just as soon, closed to the other prey that are able to move at their ease, and that, one knows not why, come thither just as soon, possibly waiting in their folly of the same kind, possibly intoxicating for the humans of the temporal life, with a body of limits, embodied. At times the Flow spits the debris of the feast in its face. For all is not assimilated to its fluid flesh, and otherwise, too lightly, leaving off in scoriae...

Having struggled against the Jialing, and vanquished since it carries it off just as soon in its own way, the Flow, voluminous, still swells, but on the other bank of the river of Fuzhou. Wherefrom it comes... These are the clear waters and good flavor. Mixed in with the life of the mighty river it brings a renewal of life both young and a little frolicking. There is a naiveté in their bounds. But what singular junks they carry or let drag over the sand... The great Flow that has no business at all with these cranky people and is already past, and henceforth, well-balanced water, short at the top of the gorges and at the top of the rapids. And that's all. The Flow is itself, complete, in possession of all its mass that throws itself in the way of the rocks.

Up to here, the apparent bone structure is supple : denouncing the deep bone structure. These are hills and valleys that are sweet enough, rejoining the waters underneath a bed that contain without shaking off. The waters course, but such is the power of the mass that nothing here comes about as in the current water. And at first, there truly is a skin on the river here ; the skin of the river.

Is it so as to better perceive the tremblings that these aquatic insects, the sampaniers of the river, hurl their little hulls at the finished planks by a very long oar at every moment ? It's undoubtedly an excellent appliance of tact and touch. Thanks to this posterior antenna, the least, the tiniest changes that the eye perceives not until long after, in the consistency, the texture, the desire or the appeasement of the water, it senses it in the same instant, and, following the time of day, reacting by a stroke of the rear oar (which they call the Sao) or by a throw of the anterior legs. But the skin of the river has quite other sensations : they fold themselves inward, creasing or dilating ; it stretches itself, fastens itself and becomes viscous, or quite all of a sudden, spins fluidly right in front of it. The wind raising the uneasiness, and testing the nerves, which it passes to recede on the epiderm ; so it crackles, makes waves (just as the sea and its coarseness and simple movements), waves that unfurl and crackle in the figure of the breeze. But these movements are foreigners, bothersome to the fluvial life. It hasn't in any way bypassed the epiderm. These are coarse excitants.

Underneath this moving skin, what an astonishing life of eddies : movements of water perfectly ignored elsewhere. There no longer are these coarse terrible fantasies that pump a junk of 80 tons straight ahead, but a whole game of discrete and incessant whirls : these spiral beings that are borne all of a sudden from the rubbing of two volumes at different speeds, organizing themselves, twirling furiously, to displace itself with a comic majesty and, if it is able, seizing on another whirl in passaging, to dominate and absorb it. This makes for an unceasing creation and a destruction, or rather this illustrates the enchainment of infinite causalities : « Of unknowing... It is not, o Master... » The Flow remembers that it is descending from the high lands of Bod whose writings still guard the pure texts of the Law and Knowledge.

Next to these whirls, other movements are coarse and a little ridiculous. These are enormous lenses, giant liquid jellyfish that all of a sudden raise up to the surface, showing their round dome for an instant, sleek, oily, and begins to stream along the edges, to spread itself out over itself in a circular soughing. These are the blows of an obtuse front, the blows of a water hammer. The more violent ones, they sometimes puncture ; and the sampaniers-men call them « water crackers » with contempt and avoid or save themselves from them since they deal out terrible vertical blows.

They know nothing but that the Flow, on the bottom, doesn't wind, but gallops like a sea-dragon : these are the momentums on inclined planes, the liquid bubbles of its momentums and its jolts.

Made of the hill bed, made of the same route, of other riffles and other adventures. The river knows how to profoundly erode the concavities of the bends, and how to round out the points by throwing all that it no longer wants there. But precisely, this turning hollow at lighting speed will be marked by new imbalances : in this extremely calm cove where the vegetal parasites, less turbulent than the humans that eat them sometimes, abound and multiply, there are inclined planes, brief and pulsatile floods, covering a rock and falling again in a cascade. There are « bad corners », a few traps, whence it is difficult to escape without risks.

These are the dissociated elements ; the scattered gestures. All this, eddies, whirls, increased speed, comes to condense to the extreme in this admirable Crisis of the Flow that is a rapids. It's a knot in the current, a decisive moment, a complete tragedy or the exposition, the crisis and the obedient unknotting to a unique décor, and which the unknotting indiscontinuously played is fatally happy and victorious.

It's in the heart of the rapid that the Flow carries to their extreme their qualities of violence, their resources, their ruses over the mountain. The rapid is the apogee of its violent qualities. Every threshold that it strangles and envelopes, every riffle is a bounding trophy. And yet the Flow seems not to know at all if it will pass through. The obstacle could be as old as the Flow itself : that's a long slope, a threshold, rocks known there by the Genie of the Flow well before the great oscillations of the opening, well before the regularization of the torrential course. But sometimes, like the most beautiful, the most pure of all, at the Hsin Long T'an, « New Dragon Rapids », it's a newly born obstacle that the same Flow hasn't eroded yet. It's a whole hill slipping over its base, and pushed into the valley by the rains.

The Flow, that for the several twenty odd years since it's existed in this place has domesticated somewhat, but it still hesitates, for two or three *li* before the pass, one sees it recollect itself all of a sudden, stretch itself out, slow itself down in a laziness that would be inexplicable, even by the depths of the basin and the profile of the terrain, if it weren't certain that the Flow, from this moment on, knows the adventure where it courses, and prepares itself for it. It knows it, and this is undeniable

; for such is this great mobile body's richness of life that it's not at all merely from the source of the opening that it moves and defiles, but at times, by the rather mysterious pulsations, that which comes about downstream is just as soon known up high upstream. From minute to minute, manifestly here, the Flow beats. That's the pulse of the rapids, the trembling before the act it must do.

And as such that, recollected, concentrated, gathered in itself, very slow in its course but already fully vibrant from the obstacle, the Great Flow readies itself for the first leap.

The surrounding rocks are high. There will be no escapes. The mountains are there to keep every velleity from detour. The Flow increases its speed, with an implacable progression ; it always beats the same rhythm but with more tumultuous jolting. From the rather unctuous course it passes to a violent run where eddies already mark themselves with eddies, soughing. If it were to look, it would see the obstacle now... but it's right here.

At the very bottom, as if a double breakwater, two rocky points launch out that clasp it. It's there where the whole lively water will pass from an only spurt. The Flow changes its character all of a sudden and here in its midst, hurled, a tongue of triangular water, polished like a lighted sword, of a hard water and without creases or by its great speed ; as a streak rushing from an implacable water.

But from the two edges, underneath, on the sides, below, the whole mass that was unable to pass to struggle, rock by rock, eddy against eddy, and to the lively tongue it's like a second bed, tumultuous with whirls. Every obstacle, every stone, every unknown riffle is a concern. From the two edges it's one indiscontinuous fringe ; the ones, descending with the central tongue, the others reclimbing the mountain to descend it in an unceasing roundabout. And the tongue, and even here the whirls come to waste together beneath the threshold, and that's the point where in a disarray without name all movements are possible. The extreme's sharpened point rolls on itself, sinks profoundly under the water's nearly vertical movement. A fringe of hissing foam absorbs it, devours it. In a sense whirls turn, others opposite it that crack it. There are projections from below to up high that come and shatter the round bowls. The

Flow, divided in the effort, crumbled, pulverized, has nothing left, no beating, no course, no conscience. Only when, at the following bend, it regains its calm, and touches its shatters, only when the speed is returned homogenous and fully balanced ; – the Flow remembers the struggle and already knows that this moment has passed.

THE MIRROR

Kyra Simone

It glistens like a star on the hillside: a giant rectangle, made up of smaller rectangles, suspended from a crane as it is transported across the horizon. Once assembled, the mirror will measure 8 x 6 meters, an expansive surface of silver glass sending back flashes of prismatic light from its edges. A crowd of onlookers watches from the foot of the crane as the panels twist from their wires in the air above. Each perilous movement is met with a collective cry of alarm. The whole village is waiting for the moment the entire fixture is installed in its place.

In the summer, the houses in this town look like they are made of wheat. They blend into the dry grasses of the hillside, a curved expanse of soft taupe roughage. Untouched by modernity, old women hobble through the piazza in brown dresses and embroidered shawls. The sun is so bright that, from afar, every person, every dried exhausted tree, the whole town, appears invisible. Now, in the middle of the day, the place is barely illuminated, lit only by dim street lamps. A banner flutters above the square. "*Benvenuto a Ombra Terra*," it says in red cake-like script. The town lies deep in the crevice of a valley, a stone's throw from the Austrian border in the Italian Alps. For three months out of the year the town lives under shadow. Being so deeply rooted in the narrow "V" between the two mountains, no sunlight reaches the rooftops of the stone houses for eighty-three consecutive days. Each November, the villagers watch as, day by day, the hillsides grow darker, until there is no light at all. It is midway through the winter now, and the people in the crowd are of a strikingly pale complexion.

In the great house at the edge of the square, a young girl lays on the floor of an attic room, two long yellow braids going down her back.

She has spread out a large towel patterned with colorful 1980's designs. She lies on it now in a garish bathing suit. Her doll lies in a similar outfit beside her, the two of them splayed out like dead fish under a heat lamp. As the rays of artificial light shine down on them, the girl puts on a pair of neon sunglasses. The glow in the window can be seen from outside, a rectangle of light that projects onto the road below. Less than a mile away, a man sits at the edge of a cliff with his hands placed on his knees, palms down for grounding, palms up for receiving. It is Claus. He is wearing patterned wool socks pulled up to his knees and a pair of sandals. There are many like Claus in Ombra Terra. They sit, a community of German Buddhists, in the same position on different hilltops, hidden away in the secluded mountain village. As the mirror glistens in the air before him, Claus closes his eyes and emits a low guttural "A-OM" over the peaks.

At the foot of the crane, out on the hill, a man named Ombro stands with a clipboard in his hands. He is the king of the town. In the parlance of these times, we might call him the mayor. Ombro is a man of a Napoleonic stature, virile and arrogant with a head of abundant curls. He goes about town with his two assistants, an eel-like pair of excitable simpletons. They stand on either side of Ombro, exceedingly taller than him, intermittently dissolving into nervous laughter, then abruptly stopping. On windy days they sway like inflatable wind socks at used car lots. Ombro is an architect. He employs many people in the town. This is why he is king. He was named after the region and comes from a long line of men who were architects before him, credited with the construction of every building on the piazza. Today, Ombro's greatest endeavor is about to be unveiled: the giant mirror he has engineered to reflect light into the town square which has, until now, remained in shadow through the winter months.

The girl with the yellow braids lies on her stomach and watches television on an old videocassette her father recorded years ago. The program is interrupted by an advertisement for a life-sized doll you can order over the phone. The commercial is in black and white. It begins with a little girl answering the doorbell to find a giant doll on her doorstep, dressed in her exact clothes. "She's almost your size," says an eerie animated voice narrating the images on the screen. "She can wear your pajamas and stay over night, too. She's as real as life." The scene opens onto a playground peopled with automated mannequins of children. One is on a swing which appears to be moving without anyone pushing it, another is standing at the top of a slide, and a third is sitting opposite the little girl on a seesaw, her eyes blinking robotically. The segment ends with a twinkling of stars and the voice exclaiming: "She's a WONDERFUL friend. She's ideal." The girl with the yellow braids looks at her own doll, now propped up on the rug beside her. Its head lolls despondently over its small body, as one cloth eye hangs loosely from its face by a thread.

In the city there are screams in the dark. No one knows where they come from or who they belong to. There is music streaming from open car windows. There are buildings that rise so high into the air that it appears as though they are floating when trains run between them on the overpasses. In Ombra Terra there is none of this. There are no cars or trains. There are no tall buildings. There are no strangers. If someone were to scream, everyone would know who it was. But they wouldn't be screaming anyway. The flora and fauna surrounding the village are remarkably tame. There are no monstrous footprints drying in the mud. The last bear was recorded to have been killed in 1792 by three hunters from Grunsveld. There are only brambles of wild berries to obscure clandestine sex acts or blue the mouths of children. All is quiet here. The lack of light is unnerving in the winter. No one talks to each other when they pass through the town square. Everyone darts quickly back into their houses, with no illuminated space inviting them to congregate or speak. The town has no stores, no post offices, or doctors. There is a single church situated on the square. A fresco of Jesus is painted on the wall outside, his skin pale as though never exposed to daylight. The holy image hangs above the basin of a fountain. A single leaking drip beats in intervals down the stone side of the concave surface.

The girl with the yellow braids climbs into a tree. She holds a pair of binoculars, her doll's head sticking out of the overstuffed backpack strapped to the girl's shoulders. There are only ten children who reside in the village, none of them younger than eleven or twelve. They are all bussed to neighboring hamlets for school. The girl with the yellow braids is six years old, hopelessly lacking in comrades her age to play with. She is the daughter of Ombro, the king. Her mother lives in America, a midwestern beauty she has only seen in pictures. Ombro has thought of sending the girl to see her, but he wonders if it will be of any use. They share no common language between them. The woman and child would not be able to speak to each other. Through the lenses of the binoculars all is in stereograph. The world they reveal is trapped inside the two circular cavities, concave and convex. The view doesn't seem real, too far away to touch, too expansive to be attempted. The mirror twinkles in transit through the air. Aside from this, the distance appears still. From the tree it is difficult to make out anything but vague shapes in the shadows that fill the valley, but beneath them the land is crawling with life. Wild ibex roam the caves above the tree line, descending to eat the succulent grasses. Bearded vultures circle the treetops, as voles hibernate in groups under the ground, building large colonies beneath the alpine pastures. Since long before the Alps were created, high-altitude salamanders have evolved among their rocks.

Beneath the snow, there are fragile under layers. The tundra of the mountainside carries enormous weight. Dinosaur fossils have been found in the surrounding peaks across the Swiss border, dating back to the Triassic era. Not far from here, glaciers have melted into rivers through forests of deciduous trees fallen and gone. Now, medicinal plants clutter the hillsides. In the darkness of the daytime, Edelweiss and blue Gentians grow in the crags of the rocks. Below the ice and sediment, Otzi works tirelessly in the forge. He clangs his hammer down onto the hot radiant copper. The malleable rod of metal partially illuminates the room. Otzi looks old for his forty-five years. He is bearded and furrowed, with deep-set eyes and sunken cheeks. His hair is full of dust, with copper and arsenic clinging to the follicles. There are bits of fresh pollen on his lips and long vertical lines tattooed down the sides of his back. His is a life of long walks over hilly terrain. It seems only yesterday that he was eating red deer meat and herb bread in a mid-altitude conifer forest, chasing wild chamois footprints through the snow. Now, on the floor of the cave around him, goat skulls decompose in the shadows. The shells of eaten grains are scattered in the dirt, flax and poppy seed, barley and einkorn, kernels from sloe fruits of the black thorn tree. A bundle of arrows leans in a corner. Soon it will be time to emerge from the cave.

"No one believed it could be possible. But I am certain. I have faith in physics," says Ombro, who is standing watch as the workers toil to hoist the mirror into place. "Tomorrow all the men in the village will be shaving in front of it." Ombro motions to his assistants to make sure they record everything he is saying. One of them holds a microphone up to him, while the other points a video camera at his face. Ombro shakes his hair out in the wind. He has ordered boxes of sunglasses to be delivered to the town, flown in by helicopter, to protect the eyes of the villagers from what he believes will be—once the mirror is properly positioned—a blinding shower of artificial sunlight. Many from town are gathered now on the side of the hill, huddled around Ombro. Others, elderly types dressed as though peasants from another century, sit in chairs in the middle of the piazza wearing sunglasses, like an audience in a 3D movie theater. The young ladies of the village are strewn about the outer staircases leading up to the stone houses on the square, wearing flower crowns and sashes tied diagonally across their matronly frocks. Everyone is waiting in pause. The Buddhists chant from the surrounding hills, each call echoing through the chasm below and joining with another voice in the distance.

The girl with the yellow braids is playing on the roof of a sunken house. She often comes here with her dog, Pico, a small Bolognese she has had since she was born. A gong strikes from a nearby cliff, as Claus sends out his prayers for the light to come. The girl with the yellow braids looks up towards him for a moment. She has never been anywhere outside of Ombra Terra. To her the darkness is normal. She doesn't know what all the fuss is about in the square. She makes her way over the wreckage of the house. It collapsed in a storm several years ago. Only the two main peaks of the roof remain above the snow, caved in and forming a wide "U" shape from end to end. In the summers, the girl roller skates between the two ridges with the dog running after her. Sometimes, they lie on their stomachs and look through the one window in the house left intact sticking up from the ground, construing haunted faces from the shadows of their own reflections. Yesterday, Pico was bitten by a wolf spider, and after suffering a violent seizure, he laid down on the kitchen floor and died. The body of the dog is stuffed in the girl's backpack. She has come here today to give it a burial. As the gong strikes again on the cliff, she slides off one of the edges of the roof to the ground and walks down to the stream on the other side of it.

Otzi steps out of the cave and looks up at the sky. It has grown a few shades darker since he last emerged. Winter has arrived and the light has now begun to slip away. In these parts, the evenings are only slightly deeper than the daytime. They hum with the smoking blue of midnight on Neptune, the sky graveled with rough grains of color. As Otzi prepares to walk out into the land, he fastens his bearskin cap to his chin. His winter cloak is made of woven grass. He wears a leather loincloth and snowshoes built from perishing tree bark and deer hide. He is often mistaken for a shepherd. Sometimes he even covers his face with animal skins to shield himself from the high winds in the snowfields. Otzi travels with many supplies, all tightly packed to his person, so that he may still maintain a certain agility as he climbs the white peaks. In the pouch sewn to his belt, he carries a cache of necessary items: a scraper, a bone awl, a bundle of dried fungus, a cluster of berries, and a fire-starting kit, with pieces of flint and pyrite for creating sparks. The quiver of arrows is strapped to his back, a mixture of viburnum and dogwood shafts, hung beside a bowstring, a flint-bladed knife, and a copper axe. The axe is Otzi's most prized possession. It is a valuable tool as well as a symbol of his status. Other men he has come upon in the hills have tried to steal it more than once. The blade is pure copper, made over many nights in the forge where he cast and polished and sharpened the axe head, then fixed it to a carefully worked yew branch with birch tar and leather lashing. As a decoy, Ötzi walks with a large bloody antler in his hand, the claw-like object both delicate and menacing, extending from his grasp like a chandelier. Today he will climb up to the rocks where the ibex take refuge before they descend to eat the succulent grasses.

Two young mountaineers trek down the hillside, with large rucksacks tied to their backs. The snow crunches into compact kidney shaped impressions beneath their feet, the only footprints for what seems like miles. One of the mountaineers is a woman, short-haired and lightly pregnant, the sort that wears a Peruvian mountain hat and teaches English in South America. The other is a man, a photographer. The two of them are on extended hiatus from their work. They have been traveling for some time now, leaving behind their lives in Reykjavík to make a slow passage to the furthest point of the Kamchatka Peninsula. They plan to move down through Scandinavia and across western and eastern Europe, before journeying the distance of the Russian territories. Now nearly four months into the trip, the couple has decided they will not return home. After they reach their destination they will keep on moving indefinitely towards unknown horizons. Their VW van, purchased in Sweden, is parked at the top of the summit that leads down to the valley of Ombra Terra, with all that they own packed into the modest rectangle of space it provides. The child in the woman's womb was conceived long after they left for their travels. She was literally made on the road, underneath a caravan parked in a driveway on the outskirts of Copenhagen, to be specific. The child will be born several months from now near Moscow. They will name her Ufa after the sunlight over the mountains to the east.

Ombro has worked a long time to make this dream possible. Stacks of diagrams sit in piles on his drafting table. Hours have been spent consulting with scientists and potential funders. Powered by robotic monitors that will follow the sun, the mirror has been designed to tilt at an ever-changing angle throughout the day, operating like a giant HelioScope reflecting light onto the square by varying degrees. There is no precedent for today's celebration. After years of lonely winters, with no one stopping in the dark square to say hello and rarely a single visitor from beyond the valley, it is Ombro's great purpose to restore light to the town.

The shadow lands are full of ghosts. The surrounding peaks have been crossed for war and commerce, by captains, pilgrims, and students alike. The crescent-shaped terrain continues far beyond the valley of Ombra Terra, reaching from the Mediterranean Sea all the way to the Adriatic and then on to the border of Bavaria. Through the centuries, the Alps have seen golden ages of naturalists, artists, and romantics. Not far from here, Napoleon led an army of 40,000 across the summit passes, and Hannibal once journeyed through the mountains with his herd of elephants. But in the town of Ombra Terra, there is no such grandeur. It is a pocket of the landscape that has been passed over by history. The girl with the yellow braids stands before the frozen stream with lifeless Pico in her backpack. A blue moth flutters through the air, descending from the peaks to drink the snowmelt. As the girl begins digging, she uncovers a femur.

Crawling through the brush on his stomach, Otzi climbs over the ridge of the peak. There, on the horizon, he sees the ibex run.

If this were a different continent a few decades from now, the Kamchatka Peninsula would merely exist as a humorously obscure territory easily won in a game of Risk. The mountaineers would announce the birth of their daughter on their website, just beside the "Make a Donation" button. There would be articles and radio shows about them, running such headlines as "Remaking the American Dream." They would copyright a name for their journey and obtain non-profit status. The man would post a running log of photos chronicling their travels, the woman would cover all the surfaces of the VW with expensive textiles and spend her free time "developing a cookbook," and it would still all somehow feel bourgeois. But for now, they are simply mountaineers on their way to see Claus, who is an old friend they met during their student days in Berlin. He has invited them here for a few nights of hot showers, and to see the unveiling of the mirror over the valley. As the two of them make their way down the mountainside, they stop for a moment to observe a wild goose in a clearing, its breast blindingly red amid the winter landscape.

All is in place for the mirror to be erected. The entire town is poised for the arrival of the light. The German Buddhists have spread through the surrounding hills, chanting collective "A-OMs" for the past hour. The crowd of elderly villagers still sit in the town square looking up at the sky, a smattering among them dozing off intermittently. As instructed by Ombro's assistants, they have adjusted their sunglasses numerous times in anticipation of the massive flash of light they've been assured will fall upon them momentarily. In the distance above them, Ombro stands on the mountainside before the mirror, the orchestrator of all provincial fanfare, sensationally enthralled by his own precious creation. He predicts that once the sunlight has been restored to Ombra Terra, there will be more visitors to their town in the few years ahead of them than there have been in the past two centuries combined.

Otzi's mind is a blur of ibex. From where he waits, on his stomach in the snow, they are as small as netsuke statuettes, an arrangement of delicate figures too far away to be thought of as living. There is a whole herd of them in the dip of the snowfield just beyond, their enormous arched horns curving all the way from their temples to the peaks of their backs. Some leap into the air, butting their heads against each other, while some sniff the ground for roughage. Others fornicate on the jutting rocks, their chins bearded like pagan icons. A few of the animals are utterly still, standing alert at the regal edges, their violet eyes staring silently into the wild. When Otzi looks at them all he can see is blood. Cartoonish visions of meat turning on a spit pass through his mind. He imagines a single stag lying on the bank of the river, a wounded mound of undulating flesh, its mouth ajar and irises red, with blood dripping from the tips of its fur into the current. Otzi pulls an arrow from the sheath on his back and sets it into place on the bowstring. As the sky above him grows another shade dimmer, he focuses his gaze on a single creature.

The girl with the yellow braids has uncovered some kind of body. It appears to have been dead a long time, a rotting frozen corpse barely resembling a man. The girl is only six years old, a mountain lass in the wild outdoors. She is not repelled by the strange discoloration of the body's outer surfaces, the patches of exposed bone, the eroded face and sunken chest. After all, there is a dead dog in her backpack. The girl is simply excited to have a new friend. The body on the ground does not look anything like the shiny dolls from the advertisement she saw playing on her father's videocassette. In fact, it barely even looks human. It has no eyes or recognizable features beyond the shape of its skull. Its upper torso juts out from a puddle of melting ice at the edge of the creek. What is left of its skin is cold and stiff. The girl with the braids drags the body out of the water onto the snow bank. Her hands are freezing from making contact with the cadaver. She decides she will call her new friend Frozen Fritz. She puts him under her arm and begins to drag him down the mountainside. At the foot of the slope she climbs up a tree, pulling Fritz with all her strength up through the leaves and arranging him on the branch beside her. Perhaps he is German, she thinks to herself. Perhaps Claus will invite them to tea. As the mirror appears in the distance dangling over the tree line, the girl wraps her arm around Fritz's shoulder. She leans her face in and kisses his cheek.

The mountaineers like to make love in adventurous outdoor places. Last time it was on the side of a cliff over a secluded bay, where the surf crashed down full of sea creatures desperately suctioning to the rocks before falling to the hot black sand below. They've also done it in the back seat of a bus driving through Croatia, and hanging from a branch on a hidden path in the Peruvian rainforest with monkeys chasing each other through the treetops above them. And there was once a simple midnight on a beach on the island of Naxos, with the deer standing frozen around them in the darkness and specks of bioluminescence lighting up the ground. Now, despite the cold and the pregnant state of his wife, the man is suddenly struck with the inclination to tie her hands and mount her against a tree.

"This has never happened since the time the world began," Ombro says under his breath, turning to the camera from his place on the hillside. The clock strikes three in the church tower over the square. The mirror is at last secured into position. All nobs are adjusted correctly. All devices are programmed and attached. But Ombro cannot see the light from where he stands. He rushes down the mountainside towards the square, and his assistants, raising sticks into the air and rapping them against their own safety helmets, holler at the crowd of onlookers to follow after him.

As Otzi releases the arrow from his bow, a set of brute hands strike down upon his back, pushing him from the ridge down the side of the cliff. It is his cousin Einarr, a rival huntsman from the next mountain. The two men fall through the gaping crevice to the field below. Einarr's body is cushioned by Otzi's, which, upon impact, lands directly upon his axe, fatally piercing Otzi's heart in an instant. It is difficult for Einarr to untangle himself from Otzi's limbs, but, after several attempts, he rolls onto his back in the snow before slowly rising to his feet. The prey has grown scarce in the surrounding hills and, having lost his own cache of weapons while ice fishing a month ago, Einarr hasn't made a fresh kill in weeks. After extracting the blade from Otzi's chest, he uses it to remove the dead man's heart. He wraps the bleeding organ in a bit of deer hide and stuffs it into his pouch, then limps away with the stolen axe in his hand. All the ibex have scattered from the field. It is the last day any light will shine over the valley for some time. With several ribs broken from the collision, Einarr falls to his own death in an ice hole a few miles away, weak with hunger and loss of blood. The sky is almost completely dark. When the sun rises the next morning, none of its light will make it down through the narrow ravine where Otzi's body has fallen.

The mob has departed from the mountainside. Everyone has descended to see the light in the square. The giant mirror shimmers alone on the hill. The girl with the yellow braids walks up to it. Her reflection in the glass is warped and elongated, making her appear much larger than she is, like an image projected onto the surface of a lake. Frozen Fritz hangs from the girl's arm, his rotten visage appearing in the glass beside her own, his decomposing body dangling to the ground. The girl is tired from dragging him across the hillside, first down from the tree and then a good distance through the valley. She pulls at the skin around her eyes and hooks her fingers into the corners of her mouth. She tries to make her face resemble his. Fritz has a Neanderthal-like countenance. His receding forehead and prominent brow ridges are thawing out and growing more grotesque by the minute. There is a snap of a branch from somewhere in the woods. It is the mountaineers, making pagans of themselves against a tree just a few meters off, the woman's back chaffed by the surface of the bark she is pinned up against. Frightened by their howls, the girl with the yellow braids runs away up the hillside, leaving Frozen Fritz on the ground behind her, his caved-in face magnified in the glass. In a minute or an hour, the insects will descend over his ocular cavities, empty craters long devoid of sight.

A single spot of light shines down on the town square. Its shape is undefined, like a spill of neon. Everything within its circumference, the empty stretch of paved courtyard just to the left of where the villagers are assembled, is illuminated. It is as though a celestial body has passed over the town, leaving a stamped impression of where it once hovered. All else is still dark. The sheep step bug-eyed from their shadowy alcoves. The people in the square look windswept and jolted. They remove their sunglasses and stand up from their chairs to gather around the patch of light. The mob of onlookers approaches from the hillside. Ombro and his assistants are out of breath when they arrive in the square, pushing past the others to the head of the crowd at the perimeter of the reflection.

A flood of thoughts is released into the air where the villagers stand gazing at the patch of light. It is as if all contemplation is caught in a magnetic field above it. One man thinks of the time he saw his wife's rear end on a moonlit evening. Another recalls the eyes of a deer in a clearing at midnight. Two older women stand beside each other in matching pinafores, the only set of twins ever recorded to have lived in the town. As they stare at the light, one sister remembers the first time she went to the cinema. The other sister thinks of death. The patch of light becomes like a hole, a glowing abyss in the middle of town into which all thought is funneled. The village slowly empties of anything but this. There is only the sun, pulsing high above the crevice of the valley. To the girl with the yellow braids, it is a giant ball of fire, one that can't be touched and can't touch you. It only reaches the earth as an idea, to change the colors of things or burn the landscape, illuminate surfaces, transform the spirit: the young woman sitting alone at the window, who sees a single ray of light cast over the floor and is roused to emerge from her dark room. The sun remains, unmoving in the sky as the rest revolves around it, oblivious to any living thing in any universe that needs it. Ombro stands at the edge of the patch of light with all the others, afraid to step into it. It is as though one would be zapped into another dimension if one touched it, transported to a land of mercury lakes, where everything beautiful becomes toxic if trespassed. Instead, he continues to gaze at the light, recalling the feeling of his boyhood summers, like the time he saw an eclipse from the top of the ridge or was dazzled by tilting a magnifying glass over a clump of ants and watching them burn through that silent stream of smoke curling into the daylight. Standing there, in the late afternoon, with the whole town frozen in the spectacle he has created, Ombro knows that he cannot be a boy again. He will never see those sights for the first time. But there are things to see that can produce similar feelings. Like this. Like the glory of erecting a giant mirror on a mountainside to bring back the light. There will be something new. Even for weary citizens who wake every morning in the same places. Even for those who sleep beside the same people every night. These are the ones who have the newness within them, who look to no other person or apparatus to bring them light. Like the eclipse and the ants under the magnifying glass, it only lasts the length of an instant.

Here in Ombra Terra, the church bells ring again. The lambs bleat in the distance. The drip of the fountain rolls down to the drain. In a house on the square a doll's eyelids flash open. A television screen turns on. A phone rings. A door slams. A finger strikes a black key on a piano. Far away in the city, a train hits the end of its track and turns right around, the conductor walking from one end of it all the way to the other, as it becomes the front again, like a worm whose tail can't be discerned from its face. In a matter of minutes the ring of people surrounding the patch of light is interrupted, as the two mountaineers drag a discolored body through the crowd to the center of illlumination. Several days from now, when the scientists examine the body with their instruments, it is determined to be a naturally mummified human from the Chalcolithic age, which, 5,000 years after its death, still possesses living blood cells.

Claus still sits at the edge of the cliff. The girl with the yellow braids hunches on her knees beside him, holding her dead dog in her arms as she looks out over the abyss of the valley. It is nearly evening. Before them is an expanse of trees shrouded in mist, with a single glimmer of light on the hillside that still barely reaches them. An array of screams rises up from the square, echoing through the chasm of the valley, so many screams that it is impossible to discern each voice that comprises the crowd. The onlookers have begun to disperse in the piazza. They are no longer concerned with the light. They have gathered instead around the hideous body, captivated by the sight as it is carted away. Ombro remains, calling out to the villagers to come back to the square. But even his assistants have been taken in by the horrific spectacle of the corpse, a presence that has been in the ground of Ombra Terra all along, through the winters of countless years before the mirror was erected, buried in the darkness below the surface. Ombro stands at the center of the patch of light, looking into the distance at his invention on the hillside.

For the first time all day, the chanting and the banging of the gongs have stopped. A "V" of red-breasted geese flies across the horizon. They ricochet against the square of silver glass, cracking the mirror into pieces.

FIVE POEMS

Ted Dodson

AN ADDITIONAL POEM

Is this the only alternative disappointment can offer?
The floor plan is as open as it's ever been,
And we ideally maintain a cinematic grief
Outside a paradise swallowing our coordinates in its own wonder.
The dead don't rise
But fall from above. I would look away
Into the room's silent reception
But as my character recedes I tire of looking at all.
The world has ended. Your resurrection eyes
Come across this second to last line—you
Can be assured I have read this already.

AN ADDITIONAL POEM

How is use fair within user-determined cruelties?
The bucket spills out empty,
And we have shadowed each other
Unknown to either of us dealing florescence.
I suddenly understood why I was even standing there
But the image didn't stick. Someone else might have guessed
Taking the appropriate channels
But like we really thought the supersize came with free refills.
The news comes to life. A rational response
Would be to quickly identify with your captors—you
Think better and get up to turn everything off.

AN ADDITIONAL POEM

What number should you call if you want to reach me?
The floor plan is as open as it's ever been,
And we shadow ourselves
Within the persistent caroling of the reservoir.
Kindness is too much to suffer
But there was a lot of repetition. We could watch the preceding
Hypothetically between two windows
But even though we get along we never greet each other.
Yard is the more appropriate term. The trees
Are in your email just in case—we
Agree this is farther than you've ever been.

AN ADDITIONAL POEM

Is it hard to believe or not?
Domestic languor pays off in its own way,
And I can't decide if I should wait
Like a head passing through the provenance of the masses.
A bit of melodrama is coughed up
But soon falls from above. I would look away
Seeing to the appropriate channels
But it was this kind of optimism that got me here in the first place.
Laughter averts a total collapse. The legislature
Is dragging a body across the lawn—I
Am assured this is definitely heaven.

AN ADDITIONAL POEM

How is use fair within user-determined cruelties?
We arrive in the middle of the night,
And our justifiable sensibilities have atrophied
Capitalizing off unexpected vacancies IRL.
A smile floats out of the elevator
But has since become routine. You know the program
As a spot in the developing sector
But history is irrelevant when we arrive in a vehicle of song.
This must be the end. The soundtrack
Delights on the remains of invention—you
Can be sure we've read this already.

TWO POEMS

Vi Khi Nao

THE MOTHER, 1985

The eloquent lungs of us twins are piled

upon one another. Mother, your

concealed nipples are the tents that the

feet of our existence step on.

I hope our breathing doesn't temporarily

upset your evening inside the tumescent

hide. This oblivion. This sublime

maternal gesture. Coming from you.

Mother, are you warm beneath the

animal hide? Does it nurture your lungs

and keep them from the cold and

sunlight?

The cane lies next to you like a stiff
husband. He is not our father, is he? Do
not forget, Mother, the recurring motif
of our neonatal breath blowing on the
crippled twilight of your neck.

The father of civilization hasn't bothered
to clothe us. The earth lives without
statues, figurines, pantheons, and
archaic stones.

Mother, isn't the night breathless? We
love being snowed into your embrace.
We love the amphitheater of your chest.
Our heads are diminutive gladiators
vying for your tenderness and beastly

lullaby.

The gods do not distinguish nature from nature, biology from science, and you haven't distinguished my brother from me. You hold us with fastened ardor.

We know that farther below us the hide is pregnant with your feet and something else we do not have a name for.

Sometimes, in the darkest hours of our breaths, I was led to believe that it was our father's bloated dead body. When we do not know what it is, our imagination runs wild.

It's lovely to lie on top of my brother's

young, soft flesh. I hope I am not

crushing his fragile lungs and bones. But

I trust you know the scales of our

existence and I trust that you know how

to balance our breaths and draw the

symmetries of my brother's body and my

body to meet the shoreline of yours.

Is this how things will be forever? My

brother's skin is so soft. Sometimes I

forget that I am not a morning glory

pressed against another morning glory.

It's just that my skin and his skin are

such amicable neighbors.

I cannot see, with your back turned

away from the dusk, if it's morning-to-be

or night. It doesn't matter, really, the

passage of time.

DAWN, 1990

They made us pull our pants down,

stretch our legs and feet, and lift up our

chins.

Five clouds wiggle like white caterpillars

that have been recently promoted to

angels.

We saw one leaf dying in the strong

rain, battered by the wind, and we

didn't stop to eat it. We let it live.

We are famous for our ability to fuck on

a string. Sexual funambulists, they call

us. The women usually fall off when we

try to fuck them. But we let them fall

anyway.

How could we save them if they don't

have legs that move like a swinging

trapeze.

[NOTE: These poems are ekphrastic studies of the figurative paintings of Norwegian artist Odd Nerdrum, from the time period of 1983–2005.]

THREE POEMS

Daniel Poppick

A COLOR ELEGIZED AS MOTION

1.

The gothic is refreshing but equally
The gothic is repetitive, in fact
It ghosts the celestial
And repetition is itself a haunted
Wood. In it this technophobe
Blossoms in spots blotted
By a constellation's viral thumb.
Luck depends on entrances—
A pink eye of the Milky Way
Catches Ursa Minor
In a mirror in the hall
And the mirror crashes
To the floor. This was our fault.

2.

I thought of you the other day
When I lugged my stuff from the sunny street
Into an empty apartment's shade
And the white walls briefly surged to green,
An optical effect duetting with the fact
Polaris stalks

From one direction, but its lesson
Is twofold: when the deed goes down
The duel is fixed
In a gangrenous room
Whose door swings on a screeching hinge,
And that prismatic shadow
Will never darken ours again.

ODOR TRISTIS

You need a big window to tattoo that trash to the back of my throat,
I've want of that sound

So bad for months
Husbanded word

In neon font
Reddening in the razored west

Fenced in letters by a feathered saber dangling from the palm.
They had it all on video. It's like hi Dad, I'm between the ages

Twenty-nine and a century, have learned to huff my company
Like nocturnes trickling through a wall.

How rare it is to truly change
One's real estate he said he said,

To change one's mold
And fold into the capitol—

I switched the lamp on off again, it's like a party in my eiessssssssssssss

Sibilant with a medium
They built a castle out of gas
I walk through, a talking prism

No lock bolted
'Twixt its rooms, a maid
Flitted inside
Collided me

And sealed herself when
My contents spilled before her
I was terrified to hear but glad

Glad to be stabbed
And let stones flow
Clearly through me
Clearly through me

The spell is consistent: you leave light to rot
And let your impediments flower by volume. I refuse to speak
In metaphors no more. Henceforth
You shall know me by my fluids: I'm Daniel,
I was born in 1914 off the cliffs of Dover. I watched anthropomorphic
        raisins sing
My father's generation's songs on Saturday morning
When sun stank and ran leporine upon
Our lawn. It almost heard
I watched and spoke in unison,
It took great pains but in my ear I know they were distinct.
I tracked the little voices as they fled the shade.
Dad was chairs
Placed there, stationary and serene.
He had these keys

THESE KEYS   THESE KEYS
Sewn into his eiessssssssssss

Spoke to me with a hinged
        Throat, opening and closing cages
Placed at the moat's mouth, or

        Chairs and space
Throughout some rooms in
        A synagogue at the bottom of
The Bering Strait.

        It was one environment
For a child, though no one accuses it
        Of being populated with a door.

The school systems were ideal
        Saddled under hydrogen
And its other double reel
        But mostly they were open.

The word we used was "temple," and some days I still do. And I've said it before, but is hungry? The city's corrective measures dissolve under my tongue. The life of things extends, it strums the room. Cars revolve around my legs, I smell Byzantium on our parachute. I shared a joke with nothing and its laughter descended from myself. Sad geist evaporated right outta my name. I'm hiding space to feel it spray my something something. For words are a shirt, and Reverend Spring sweats through it. I approach him after mass and slash triangles upon his book. He accepts that invitation with some grace, his skin stretched over its frame bleeding a general yellow. He then uses a wood to nail his young body to his studio. I walk to the edge of that plank. I have choices,

The road to Epping being paved with brooches
Flattened under wheels of
"Limos have a way of reminding you that all of life is about
Perspective. Like we discount everything that disagrees with history.

Living in Israel I can relate to that, you got these
Optical illusions.
Which makes peace a whole
Lot harder,

Because it attaches people to identity as a sense of *turth*.
That's why I'm
Excited for you who see the information of my legs
And share it thusly, like John Clare weeping into this stretch ride,

Gangrenous paper beeps upon your shelf, I mean
You're only recognizable as yourself."
Observe thy happy, humble load
And prevent it from prophetic cells.

"And banish from Man's life his happiest
Life," quotes E___ from John Milton. It makes me
Feel kind, wanna spend the forsythia,
Carry a cartoon horse into a lake on my back. His face mopes

And his melting voice is braided with a flock of zeroes
Flapping at its seam.
"I can't seem to feel the hammer when you morning,
Or I guess the polite thing would be to ask you do you morning? Because

Most of them flash all afternoon, mouths agape with structured rain
Pouring out
In film with no footage and just as loud,
My father's face a scribbled cloud."

IN THE NEW MUSIC I'VE DISCOVERED NUDITY

When the fox sinks into the rock
The poem speaks for the fox
When the poem sinks into the rock
The rock speaks for the rock

TWO TEXTS

Steven Seidenberg

The Imperium of the Stimulus

for Bill Berkson

To let nothing show of the true affair, one must tell the true affair. One must allow signification to make seignory—to make *of* seignory—the simple of a surface, of an outside *looking in...*

φ

Why must *perception* be propitious to the dreamed simultaneity of worlds intrinsic to it? If we renounce all ready purpose, do we not forsake the necessity of such renunciation? Why must we abandon the teleology of history simply because its function as a cipher of *encompassment* means that it must end, that it must be concluded with the balance of its absence... of its precedence as absence, just the same? Why, finally, must we cower from what *disgusts us...*

φ

What cannot be remembered cannot be endured. Meaning is a form of interruption, a pause in the imperium of the stimulus...

φ

If the being of beings is determined—is *understood*—by some associative reflex; if the existences of *particular* things—of things that somehow terminate—are discerned by virtue of a faculty intrinsic to the knower—distinguished, that is to say, by some appurtenance interior to the faculty of discernment—then how adduce the structure of that demiurgic organon by looking from a distance? How think to take the measure of the faculty of measurement?

And how, dare I say, map the interior of one's own occluded oculus by searching for a sight line, for the succor—of a *surface*…

φ

We are not only superfluous to nature, but to the destruction of nature. Even our denials are in league with natural law…

φ

Such simpering betrays us. Everything lingers past its use. We find traces of fairy tales in shopping lists. On every log, a toad. When one apprehends the moment through its *coming* recollection, the haze clears. One knows how it will *seem* to have lost *this* time; how one will take account of something so much *less* than memorable; the pain of a loose tooth; a glint on the sea…

φ

Desecrated windows offer static views; the diffusion of light confuses everything. There is only one image in the end; in the end, there is only one image…

Ward

The field is empty. The games are done. Nothing remains but festival rubbish, all streamers and munition shells. This is where we go, after the fun has ended. This is where we find ourselves—the ditches wide, the mud still warm. It is a good place—and everything is good. To hide in holes already searched—the essence of wisdom...

φ

When the future rises up as clear as a sewer grate through a foot of water and the protean mull of humus sticks to a hole in your shoe like a stare, you have surrendered to the privilege of suspecting everyone, of supposing everything an image worth the forfeit of its forfeiture, the truncheon of a prurience made commonweal...

φ

Repetition is not delirious; before the advent of desire the body is bespoke. That the tailor is hardly a craftsman, that one's vision of the future—of the absence *filled*—is no more than a vector in the project of transcendence, means that no satiety completed can project itself towards anything but recapitulation...

φ

The art of denying without making inimical; the art of destroying without *making space*...

φ

No aberration—*as* aberration—is worth anything to one's attempts to reach repleted acumen, nor one's parallel concussion into plenary array. A gathering of exiles reveals character only insofar as it is character *in common*; as there is something in the aggregate that forms the very *choosing* of the many who are proffered thus as augur, or as ward...

φ

Yield to the charm of catastrophe—the climax of a certain convulsion; this is your door to the new way, this is the new way inside the old. Retreat in step with common faith, the topos of a certain void can't hold you back, can't see you through. This is what you *can* do, what your peevish path to dispatch coalesces from the molder; this is where your triumph lies, don't doubt it...

φ

If I were silent I'd hear nothing. No time for inflection. If the pauses are not endless, then they have not really happened. What right have I to stop even a moment? Only the dead have rights, but there are other forms of warrant...

φ

The far-away begins by being within sight. One must at minimum discern a certain outline in the distance for the distance to have meaning, for the promise of the harbinger to differ from mere faith. If some consummate conceit is made to seem a final purview, if the time for second guessing is to come around...

φ

There is no behind to the image that conflates the world with substance, with the silence of substance; that the vestiges of voice remain indentured to the project of elision makes of every ear an address, but only for those speakers who have managed to conceal it, who have opened to the promise of *their own* excise...

EXCERPT from *COIL*

Lou Pam Dick

If to start one step ahead, wrong step, the nix is a beginning. I wore my stairs around my neck, therefore I choke. Please be legible. What time is it? The door keeps opening. My *protector* gets all wet. I shout, I am my bodyguard! I whisper it inside me. Bare the neck of the child traitor: Edmund. A snow descends. This can't get any air now. Red outside, white inside. A black edge to finger, balance on. The fingertip (index of name) is split and flapping open. It moves, while chirping indicates a sewing. Secret stitches: red. My *bodyguard* heats up. I shout, I am my lifeguard! I whisper it beside me. Orange to fold into. Light and shadow cut across the things, deform them. To be slathered onto the world, its convolution of shocks, nicks, springs. Why won't my hand obey me and be legible? Its lines break. It isn't night, it's day. The rise/ruse of meanings. Please take your hand out of my book. The writing *is* the being or becoming. The life without, detritus. Or that same candy bar wrapper, flapping through: a Betwixt bar. Two as oneness. A blackness in your neck. What flickers into nature. The hearing on the grass. A numeral 3. When very slowly. Liquids pouring out of everything. Not a blood envelope, nor a phlegm envelope, nor a yellow bile envelope, but an ink black one. Full of messages. The recurrences. We float inside our liquids or we are them. What Ed dripped onto his paper sheets. He is my seventh-grade boyfriend, Johnnie. I am Johnnie; I have small hazel eyes, dark blond straight hair, small bronze boy nipples, a small slim body. I am St. Johnnie the Small (for God), until I become Edouard Ton Petit, with little mountains. Women have bald spots visible from the view from above. My hair is thinning and falling out like a man's or woman's. The vortex, swirl, at the back of my head. It's vexatious. Their fontanel, my whirlpool. A pale blankness of meaning at the center. There is no ground, but there is sky. There are no feet, but there is crown. Skull cap, pen cap. When it does not become language, and the plants are drooping. I smelled the other world, and it unearthed me. Dark twin earth, its evil twin. A jejune frankness plays both sides now. Not the shiny pen that could play Ed Rusher if not the Stalker. The island in the sea, seen from above. Or to possess your own solitary island. Floating in the oceanic language. Seen from above, a map, a pattern; seen from within, an amp, a clatter. Or a lung flap. My chest *protector* is a flapper. The things become too moist and shred, turn useless. To be above or slightly to the side. My body muffled in black and blue. White feet of floating saints. Or yesterday's lead legs when running away from the asylum. *This* is the motion in stillness. Girls should sit with their logos crossed. Now picture the blue Erector Set. Its red case. Or green man-uscript with pink illuminations. Ashes died and had to be buried. Birds bark and dogs chirp. I was a dog-bird once, when I was Mina the prodigal daughter, but these aspects weren't recognized. Return to that or swipe it. Heat under skin. My perpetual burning, sweating. Johnnie the Humid Torch. Hell as an internal onesie. Or what your metal skeleton can do to you. Why the thoughts hang off you, flaccid thought skins. Forehead skins. A pelt as place to hide inside or pelt the world from/with. See stoning. Or the black smooth one, shape of seal, except it had some tiny scratches. Your fate took another place. That was before this. Heresy or tower. After fall down or out, unwrite. *Unground* of Boehme the Bohemian. Mercury of rhapsody. Clinical, unsanitary. Sanctity of titties. Free the hair, a shock. Do not repeat that? The words keep flowing from my nostrils, like the vapor of bold horses. Anaximenes, Anaximander: pre-secretions. Plato rode them. I have no doubt that there is spirit. Therefore to be spirited away like a Japanese animated movie is a good. Or some *apeiron* suture. Whaddup, stitches? Orange tones layer up. The back of my neck/beak exposed to the elements of Euclid. They seek safety in white mechanisms, numbers. I deny the poem as machine, say it is a current. Electricity of fluidity producing sparks. (Electri*city* of God, or I am an Electri*city* girl, or Electra*city* of *you rip PDs or Sufferglees*.) I am not interested in mechanical parts or how they fit together. Paint is fluid, ink is fluid. Once they called me Vincent of Go, or Her of St. Victor, or *einfach* Herlderlin. I will cut off my left ear when I can't bear its ringing anymore. In fact, I already depicted it in an incomplete painting which was meaning as abstracting. Fracture. My *secret* name is ineffable, though; I wear it under my crotch. Clothe yourself in white or blue or thought stripes. Some rise and some turn sideways. Not above, nor below, but off to the outskirts of side dishes. Yet truth was an ascendant. Or is it no longer the vertical, rather the marginal/*gutteral?* Detachment wrinkles the hand. Long fingernails and toenails need slip covers, but I still wear them to honor Holden Nils, just one of my small blond boyfriends here. Paint under, not over, the nails. Manny PD: a little big man. A girl cuticle. I know too much, I am eight years old, I am smiling under my bangs, I am a mischievous smarty-pants, and Mama photographs me. Or else Papa does, while Mama sheds her cleanliness, her prefix. Her smile fell down and broke its shoulder. Do not let the violet sadness flower, beep.

———

10:28

Between hither and thither. Running yourself into bricks: how the red could tattoo you. Putting on your skin in the morning. It has grown baggy, misshapen. Preparing to join the vagrants in the park, not the lost park/childhood, but its darker twin, east of Eden. Is there more than one mountain, peak? Your thoughts become a sex mob, flow job. The paper unable to absorb all the liquidity, or else it stains it. Therefore blot it. Inking, marking, snacking. Like Gus of Painting (who, like Plato, loved horses platonically), not Gus the Saint (who, like Plotinus, loved the One). Spraying language over everything? No, world gushes out through hose of language. I eschewed lingerie, but I chewed on lingering. Buster Keaton doing Bartleby. Still, a coiled form, like a snake, might dart its tongue and know things. Coil = girl + boy + speed of light as current. Moving between here and there, between tower and asylum (what was *its* architecture?). Fascination with the forms of buildings yet not/not yet systems. Her liquid romanticism. The relation of liquid and vapor. Solidity is *ganz* uninteresting. Fissure, paper, cock. Suture, paper, crack. Don't play *that* pubic game again! I have tics, I have old lie disease. Wearing a childhood that leaves your wrinkled inner forearms exposed. Shredding middle-aged for everywhere. A feral child, an immature old lady. The curled bag lady you keep seeing, who is eyeing you. Her line humbles your dissembling, quells your thumb's drive. This will inevitably lead to that. Reductive, not deductive. Nor seductive. Is that also a tower? The tower of heresy. Of hairy seeing: Gus's conversion. Or the other Gus, or Ludwig. The conversion narratives compel me, but they aren't narratives, they're aspect shifts, or if your eyes fell out, and then you touched things. Once upon a time, I had one. It's my secret, I am wearing it as a there-shirt, under my here-robe. It isn't quite a bathing suit, although the sea of air allures me. Then my top, a sort of black bandage, came down, and my breast saucers were in the elements. My friend today is Carl Seelink, aka Clink. The clink is also the cell, aka the slammer. The little house was moved to the country, like a mad writer to an asylum: is that my per-fected future? The dishonesty of repetition versus the truth of variation, or the honesty of repetition versus the myth of pure invention. The *lie* is how there's functioning. One brick red tower, one dark red tower. Fire, blood? Don't think about yourself as a roaming Ziploc snack bag filled with two-toned liquid. But without liquidity, there's only death. The struc-ture (bone, muscle, nerve, vessel) not availing. Electric liquidity prevailing, unveiling. It could inhabit another form. So *can* machines think? But it needs consciousness, sensation. My sensational yellow journal to Maeve's hysterical red novel. May + Eve = Maeve, as in Maeve Rocker. She is the queen of the fairy kingdom, with the king, her husband, Ernest Yonder. (All the mad ones such as Hölder need their serious *protectors*. Who pro-tects the hunched old lady?) Or your ear's nest, how it's nesting in your room. How the birds of sounds grow up in it. A tower in the ear is said by rain. Or how it grows, becomes fleshy, gross, revolting. Like Ed Atkins's. His shaved head, skinhead pathos, and his liquids, seeming queerness. He didn't know or hear things. Various cocks I'd like to slide on but keep out of me. Their quivering urgency, their pre-come, their angled rigor. Versus flowing, coursing errancy. My exposed head, no longer protected by my shocklocks or my helmet. She and I have helmets. She is a child queen, except she is much older and my Mama. No. She is a virgin queen, despite whatever enters her. Nevertheless peace is elusive, not a conqueror. So her name is soluble. The fear hairs, the few left on the skull, or a shapeless rug flung across it. But it grows from it. Still, it is time to reread the *other* man and to varnish/cherish him. Versus enamel finger painting, its lucid smoothness. Or the nails again. A tightness in my underchest (she wrote *overbra*!) from anxiety, regret, or a superabundant surging up of liquids. They were stains, and spilled over into each other, and got called *female*. The girl awakening to find herself *verwandelt* into an off-white stain on the sheet. Of some dubious night-time liquid. A god-shaped pool? A holy pool? A girl-shaped puddle. Therefore it is I, not my brother reading Franz. In fact, this time, I have no brothers. I have said everything I would ever need to say about brothers and etc., yet I keep inking, speaking in pings (if I'm using my Hermès 2001 or my Underworld 222 and not my Japanese red or Japanese black pen. My method is a secrecy.) My compulsive obsessive disorder (a cod piece) keeps making clangs, pings, gongs. Like Henri! His plangent slices. There are some with whom I will never be done. The free-form swings its arm. Last night's noise was Japanese no wave/free jazz in Martian-style asylum! Form as liquidity, not liquidity as formless. A formalist infusion. What is the form of truth? The formlessness of Godhead? Rethink the designs of stains, of coil spills. Don't be coy; be coil. A hank like Hank Errant (homing hero) or a spiral backnote? Not daxophone or dictaphone, but helixphone. One day I shall turn leaf, though. And aloof.

———

11:22

She scratched my rock, my black rock, my oblong seal rock, my fingerling, do not scratch me! Back then I was a seal, and then my feet were, they were shiny, sleek and black, shy but not unfriendly, magical creatures in the water. Or my sleek smooth small black head and large dark eyes and pronounced snout. Or the seven seals, Bergman and the apocalypse. Or my lips are sealed, so I am a seal on the go-go. They are quiet and inviolate. While Nola (unless Nuala pronounced Newla) is my *protector*. Once she was a bear and I was a Japanese girl that balanced on her big warm paw as she lay on her back, holding me up, inside our slowly unfurling, glowing scroll.

Clipped cord, interruption of connection. Movement of the blue sphere of head. (Cobalt or cerulean.) Vibration's space cap. Fitting in to a pre-determined space or making one. Removal of a grid. The rumblings at various frequencies. Whistle of the bird work. A gap a cat could fit through. White dots on orange square, increasing in size while rising. A foreign language wafts leftward. Words hang down from the balcony. Lines transect a void. Could you write from joy again? I am a black seal, I am shiny! A tall man's calves. One nuzzled a teat. The black sheep not metaphorical, it's little. Horse in facemask. Blue and yellow walk together across a street. Humans cannot bear the brightness. A hot sweat of the spirit, from the inside. One way street walker. Closely shaved head. Hands that dangle out of shirt sleeves. A sleeve tattoo could be a form of knight's election. Flowers or higher powers. Not to be burned at the stake, despite my clairvoyance, cross-dressing. A woman limps. The mechanical is close to the organic, biological. All the girls with bangs. Reunion with the deer/dead found in a dream. I dyed my hair yellow with black roots. I didn't dye it, I will never dye it, I am too lazy. Also the school blackboard that was my governess/nurse told me not to. It was God who dyed it. To be a vagabond for God. To be St. John the Small or a book lady. But the word *lady* is repulsive, unless appliquéd to Nola, my *protector*. I was planning to become a small bent Chinese man in my old age, now the something will not let me. There's no *permission* to be joyous, but there is an *obligation*. Contradiction! Violet trickles down, green spurts up. The one who sang of birds on a wire warbled close to here. He was a cone named Lionel. No, I am a coil named Lionel! Death gently fingering the petals, their pale whitish-yellow. A certain coldness could keep you away. Or the dualism of the language of some horror stories. Being *tested* in your youth with Rorschach inkblots, for precocious signs of insanity. No thought is now writing me. Once, a doll's house offered tiny boxes of dry cereal, tiny desk lamps, tiny carpets. To be a building versus to be the humans in it. I do not feel human. I was a building once. I was two buildings. They were

Modernist. Red and pink pieces of cardboard also fit into each other to create a temporary dwelling, as if for all the immigrants. The childhood is more real than the adulthood now. I slipped through a fissure in the now-plane, went to another now-point. All times exist at once as plies. They're stains, are layering? The most complicated colors. That lady painter and her husband painter. He philosophized, she stained things, they said. My left hand has been amputated. I lived halfway in a fairy tale that ran with colors. Please reread that. There were always two companions, now there are two companions. Like the two birds here. My eyes hurt from trying. My eyebrows hurt from forgetting. Metallic planes clang, and the flock streaks. Nervousness stalks me. My stalks waver, I am growing up nervous. I did not grow up, I grew sideways. Now I am a blotchy manuscript illumination on the world book of God. I am a marginal doodle, offering no deeper insight, no pointed instruction. I am a coil, looping around in a Beatus manuscript, or some other. I would like to be blessed for my design, my special formal properties. Is such innocence permitted? People laugh at me or they disdain me, I accept that. Can an experienced girl still be a holy fool? I grow sidelong more foolish every day. I forget things. I no longer understand things. When I replace my parabolic watchman's cap with my conical dunce cap, God will select me. He will click on me to give select's erection. Foolscap is a kind of paper that's stained with a liquid mark in the form of a dunce cap. My name is Johnnie/Lou Marker. My folio remains inviolate, unshown.

—

10:10

It was the yellow-green of light, the beacon. Now I am deinstitutionalized. The hydraulic lift of my ladder is still sleeping. The climb into Plotinus. He was small, black and green, his corner folded just like mine. An organ opens. What to make of the flow of mental traffic. The speed bumps in my way, my oath. They said route, I said truth. A shiny black fly on the edge of the phenomena. A phenomenal array that is a clothesline with wet adjectives. Interchange of sensitive or bodily currents as epiphany. With Hölder, Ed, Eva, Nola, or etc. The sideways slant of my attention, its indecency. Or diagonal unguent. Coils lighting up now, sparking hot! The back of your head flames, and the back of your neck flames, and there *is* no past.

———

Noise that slices through. Why are they always cutting things? I removed my nylon sheath, my prophylactic garment, my nervous system's condom. I said it before (I have said everything before): the sole worthy system is the nervous one. Orange cube of the past stood on the other side. I could no longer fit/feel into it. It wore a white yarmulke and a white mouth guard. A tall man such as my father went into it to drive it. It stands for ancient fluids, obsolete ways of maneuvering. A dulcet clanging lies at my feet, its paws extended. I am alone; others have company, but I have this constant ringing on the left of me. To jam something into the ear or to be fucked there. I said this in *The Prodigal Daughter, aka Parabola*. Is the One too small for me to fit my current swollen head into? It's time for another tonguing. I learned to play the clarinet so I could become a moat's art named Wolfgang, then I turned into a lacy crown named Steve. Some number is a black code on a yellow dickey. Yellow appears everywhere; it is *the essential*. The black arrow points down on the mountain, as if to say descend first. But the icon is a combination of spread thighs, sharp cock. I am a hermaphrodite, my name is Hervé Rocket, that is quasi-sonic, I am not a quiet writer. A rocket combines the shaft and head with the slit, goes beyond mere distaff. Lack of testicles a boon. If I were lying with my legs spread and my small penis erect, upward on my belly, it would look exactly like this arrow with its base of pronged tail (snake's tongue) on my dark Plotinus book. Is he my green/black mentor? Is he empty or a mountain? The mentor is the shaft between the head and the tail: >mentor>. Flames are arrows. Fire of iteration at the back of my neck, the groundwork of my skull. Heraclitus says the origin is fire. The vulnerability I always try to protect there: it is a heat. I am a new American library or a unity in Montreal at the disloyal collection. A free mangirl translates the Vorsokratiker, I am a post-Socratic fragment unless a thread dipped in unguent, a yarn dipped in tallow, Descartes' wax flowing into this, but now it is time, again, for Søren Kierkegaard, and this little book was first printed when I was about to become one of the One. My rightness is not reserved, my writing is copying, and my essence is a dubbing/doubling, enhancing bootbling, sequins of sequences, and the essential is the return, the greatest pleasure, and my father's signet ring is the one I kiss repeatedly (*he* is my mentor, but I am the mentality of my mind), he is Barnabas and I am Antigonix, I am a non-representational treatise or set/series of treatises from the unneeded, and my *protector*'s name is Nola, but she still lets my neck burn. Now it's time to bare my arms.

———

11:01

The park across the way is Unedenic, not the twined square nor the washed square, not la jeune minx, but it is the set of singletons, idiolectical azures that are soaring, and I hover at its edge, not inside it, but slightly higher and observing.

Men's voices enter me, and it does not hurt for once. They reposition their metal pipes, their metal structures. A lost language arises in bursts. Do not let the beauty burn you so it hurts. Must I *still* protect myself?

———

9:17

It waits and waits, then it erupts. Why can't I *see* things? The feeling of inadequacy is furred. Something judging me. Yesterday's blond man, facial stubble but small puffy Jesus tits on his husky chest. The joy of playful Carl. An emptiness billows out. The whole Erector Set unpurchased. The structure (web of nodes) tearing from my anxious fingers/figures. Harlot's web, but the *true* madness was a lack of phonic wordplay. This is a lie which I pasted to my yellowed belly. No label means the self does not create itself. Against German Romanticism's circle, her mad romanticism's coil. Its abject errancy. A stem of cell. A lie and a sadness.

Madness wandering, unable even to specify a foodstuff. The phantom of the 1001 plateaus. Take apart the cheaper structure. My backward glance against the wall. Where is my breast plate when the bullet points are shot at me with their uncanny powers? I dress up like a *bodyguard*, a detail of security, but all is thin, uncertain, even the shadows tremble with fear. The past flattens me, and the fissure in my chest organ oozes lava, pre-come, spit.

My life as shining veil over abyss.

My notebook slaps me.

———

2:04

A bent light vibrates. What sticks the ivory pages: a mistake. As if a stem. Colored spheres coalesce. My bare arms get held back. A little girl sobs. The information a dissimulation. Thoughts cluster under roaring militancy. The bursting thought balloon. Inside the void, a hallway. Cornered subjectivity. A girl is causal, claustral. Thought of the German collar turned up. The names crawl across the higher plane, individualism flowing under, at different speeds. Perched in the childhood chair (orange and silver) over the *Unground*. Intensity frays the crotch. A collection felt stifling. Incompleteness of how you demand to be left off the list. Then mathematics haunts you. A curved, knobby spine in off-white vulnerability. Obscuring the sign with foliage. Why can't this expose the meanings? An improvisation droops. Green, red, yellow, white. Green time skirts the crystalline. The voices coil around. Inside the blossom of sexuality. Pale yellow stain on green of newness. I felt *unglaublich*. A secondary sex character spills over/ into, like a language. The hair stands up when it ends. Parisian breasts are pastries that have spoken. Streetsmart Sainte-Catherine whirled away the time through paraphilosophy. What does *cat* say? Chantal Akerman called me feline in a hallway once. A calico cat or fabric lay on its side, extending holy pauses. Let the nib gently touch the rectangle, the silver annotate the black. Without the rose of lining. Or the ruse of living. A one-piece philosophy that was called a leaper. To read would be less vacuous. The cables cross in perpendiculars but also in diagonals. Parallelism in Spinoza, parabola in yourself. To philosophize through a surface. A false frontality around my neck, a falsely thrusting forwardness. To choke or hang yourself (with hanky pain key). What is absent from your truth-shirt. The truth/death that still pursues me. Truth as dybbuk? Haunt, honte. Frank shame of -phone's translation. While the abstractions do not make it past the ants today. All instants of writing are antsy twilights, *pure* night or day stays silent. Transvaluation of tones' chest valves. Or a vulva drawing. Though St. Paul Klee could teach me now, or Sir Josef Albers. Then my disheveled alp hair plays shallow ditties, and Hermes von der Alb was an otherlocus. Is the being collared by a new German girl a sign of former Inga? Or is the new Eva/life still a possible value of the x? Arranged domain. What doesn't function as connective tissue falters. All the nodes as if a net, but I still say the form of spiral. Looping forward or around. Or gagging on one's ending. Once I wrote *The Folie of My Marker*, but I wasn't truly mad yet.

———

7:05

Lost an hour to the dream of a man in a movie masturbating (in his pants), then full erection (still in pants) aims at camera, about to ejaculate onto lens, I woke up, climax. In real life a woman performer on a stage: a dancer. What? There is a different bird near me. No, it's gone now. It was a dusty brown dove, I moved slowly so as not to frighten it into flight, but the erection scared it off. I lost the dawn hour, is the day ruined for me? Yesterday was meant to be Chinese and natural, how the painted ones retreat to cubes on mountains, but it became about the viscous physicality of paint, dissolution of the safely human in the Austrian alien, all is tactile energy, and how the colors splat, dissolve you. Yellow, pale green, ochre, rose, dark purple, a scratch or two of black. What is a body? The normal modes of being, communication now repulse me. I became dirty in my lubricants and boisterousness, my upbeat words and handwriting jobs. I want to find another language, quit my joking. A black vertical semi-circle strolls down a street. The world gets delivered in black and grey, with pink Latin tying its hair back. That assertion is stupid, meaningless. How to become truthful again? The sunlight hits the window down the block, reflects and blinds my eyes. My day is now posthumous, with precocity.

———

7:27

Could you raise the world in a New York minute, or does God raise it in the blurred out *Instant?* I spent 40 seconds in the desert, being flooded with lights or doubts or human temptations. I keep trying to become like the others, but I think I am not human anymore, I am parahuman. The downstairs dry cleaners today made their car into a silver lining in the blackness: how is that possible? There is so much I don't understand. Prince Myshkin minus the constant, beautiful compassion is just a klutzy idiot. Return to the idiocosm? I am not in the mystical stage because of lacking the divine charity, the prerequisite. A woman was begging for meaning, I shook my head before she had even finished her question, I felt her disgust, I am disgusting, while she is still a hungering. Therefore God subtracted his shimmering, tactile, painted Austrian epiphany from me. A band of grey, a band of green, a band of lit-up pink, a band of baby blue that emptiness might reel. Too much sensation and not enough thought can kill a girl. But mostly they're killed differently. Do not be at the address of that, you aren't worthy of it either. But is my truth mere fantasy? Trash and voidville *sans* connections, glowing separately. Then a new banner of pink meaning, a hanging signcloth. Now paint the leaves of yellow particles. I am trying to ampersand yet to withstand, to sidestep almost everything.

———

7:10

If to burn in fingers.

How the yellow goes too far, then it must inch backwards.

The birds all on one side now, with the singing. While my eyes blur.

Do not look down into the void/abyss you border.

Men's shorts/shouts do not stop time.

Too late for quiet.

White moon against pink cloud, blue sky was cancelled.

Putting on, then taking off the vision.

Curling your back.

The birds as apex, not foundation.

Or the roof is the foundation. Of God's mouth.

Willful one-sidedness of my approach, when the truth must be two-sided. Or n-sided?

Rhythm of larger containers among the smaller.

Blueness growls. An olive man as manuscript illumination.

Exposing yourself with one tit and a foreign language.

Last night's dream of the building (an auditorium) shaking, about to collapse, and you had to get out, climb out, but then as if through a window in an adjacent building, and an Eastern European or Slavic little blond boy was helping you, telling you how. (Your body an enigma, hindrance, an unusable.) Fear, and looking back toward the trembling building.

You cannot *acquire* the Holy Ghost, take it in your hands. It has to take you.

Liquid trash conditions adjacent to me, in droplets: they splash onto me.

I meant truth conditions.

The cries of birds indescribable in adjectives.

The tree across the street, with its naked body diagonal, leaning over the street.

German birds line up on the scuffed matte blackboard of the cornice. They chirp, *Ungrund!*

Underground lockers for implorers only. Or was that the ground floor? Many corridors infect/inflect a schoolgirl.

Write the *other* dream, the new revelation. But that would be to miss the brown leaves falling.

The clouds like diagrams, to show topologies. But I am nowhere with geometry.

Through the window's stitches, its slit screen, I see the surface called *the world*.

PAN AND HOOK

Adam McOmber

Do not imagine me nymph, nor fey, nor ragged spirit of the air. I am a stranger body still: fine and silver-horned. Once, I walked on burnished hooves through the leafy shade of unspoiled Arcadia. Shadows of lush fir spilled over me. I carried a flute of tethered reeds. And there was always music. Or at least the memory of it. I tripped from stone to stone, sometimes pausing to pick lice from the fur of my hindquarters. My mind was quiet, stilled by trees and streams. But in my heart there hung a kind of longing: a heavy, dripping nest. It was difficult to name all the creatures that inhabited the nest. I could only say that I knew they would never leave me. And I, in turn, would never be permitted to take my leave of them.

How many a handsome soldier did I frighten on those long-ago forest paths? Men, in the dusky light, grew startled at the sound of my music. They claimed they glimpsed a pair of lamp-lit eyes. They heard a violent rustling. There were stories told about me around the campfire. The Beast of Parnon stalks us, they said, the goat-god of the wilderness. And yet, I meant those young Romans no harm. In truth, I longed to hold them, to comfort them. I wanted to kiss their full Roman lips and stroke the hard white scars on their shoulder blades.

I remember one dark haired boy, a youth whose name I never learned. I chased him into a copse of Alder trees. He trembled. And then he prayed.

"What have I done?" he said. "The gods—the gods are angry."

I attempted a gentle expression. "I am not angry," I said.

The boy fell to his knees. He shook and wept. Later, I learned he drowned himself in the Tiber.

*

There was an earlier age, of course, more rustic and more faith-filled. I was worshipped then. Priests made sacrifices in my name. Pindar writes that the virgins sang of me. They called me Ba'al and Tammuz. They wailed and struck their breasts. In truth, the songs of virgins did not interest me. Instead of listening to their paeans, I would climb the barren mountainsides. And in the darkness there, I'd teach handsome shepherds to touch themselves in nighttime fields. I instructed those men how to soothe one another. How to kiss and be kind. I remember the scent of the herdsmen, flesh and sweat and leather. They lay together amongst the broken pillars of long-dead civilizations, wrapped in one another's arms. They were satisfied, clear of eye. And that, to me, was worship. That was praise.

*

But there are no longer any shepherds on the hill or Roman soldiers in the wood. Man is a fool for time. And always he abandons his gods. Here is how I too was abandoned: One morning, a sailor called Thamus—not a particularly beautiful or interesting boy—was on his way to Florence. Near the coast, he heard what he believed to be a divine voice coming over the water. The voice, in haunted tones, said: *Pan is dead. Proclaim it. The Great God Pan is dead.* I was in the forest when I heard the echo of those words. I listened all day and into evening, hoping for some refute. But the wood remained silent. And I knew the incantation that the voice had spoken was somehow true. The boy, Thamus, repeated it in village and city: *Pan is dead. Pan is dead.* The dreadful words, over and again. And Pan *was* dead. As was Ba'al and Tamuz and even the Beast of Parnon. I was left a nameless thing. Forsaken.

*

I retreated to an island then, a bleak outcropping in the sea. It was a small enough rock to have no name. White lilies grew from its crags, and great storms sometimes welled. I took no interest in such things. I did not play my pipe or gambol along the shores. I hoped only that this place, this empty Never-Was, might be a vessel strong enough to hold my grief. I told myself I must learn to feel at home on the cold island. For I too would "never be" again. I found a grotto. I slept in a cave near a pool of black water. And there I did not dream. For what would be the point of that?

And then one day, many years after my arrival on the island, I heard a clamor upon the sea. There was shouting, and there was canon fire. I scuttled from my cave and perched upon a stone to watch two great ships do battle in the island's narrow cove. I saw fire. The ocean itself turned dark with soot. And after a long while, when one ship had sunk and the other had sailed victorious, I slunk back to my cave, wondering whom the dying men might have prayed to in their last moments.

It was then, on the rocky rim of my home, that I saw a smear of blood. The blood smelled human. It smelled male. My heart quickened. I peered into the darkness of my cave and discerned there a shape: a man, hunched and shivering. I realized he must have been one of the sailors from the sunken ship. He'd somehow dragged himself here from the sea. The man was handsome, dark, wearing a red coat with buttons made of gold. His black hair dripped with brine. The pale fingers of one hand trembled on his knee.

I crawled toward him in the darkness, hoping not to frighten him. The sailor, perhaps the captain of the sunken ship according to his regalia, bled. He'd been wounded in the battle. There was a deep cut on his cheek. And his left hand, I realized, was entirely missing. It had been hacked away. Yellow bone, hook-like in its shape, protruded from the meat of his wrist.

The sailor opened his eyes when he heard my approach. It had been so long since I was close to a man, since I'd smelled a man's scent and felt a man's breath. I realized, in that moment, how badly I wanted this sailor. If he would not worship me, at least he might know me, make me feel as though I continued to exist. To my amazement, he did not recoil at my approach. Instead, he smiled wanly. "Peter—" he whispered there in the darkness of the cave. His lips were bloodless, nearly white. "You're covered in dirt. You've been playing—the river."

I said nothing. For I was not, nor had I ever been, called "Peter." And I did not know what river he spoke of.

"I'm sorry," the sailor said. "I'm so sorry." He winced in pain. "I've wanted to tell you—so many years—I sailed—"

I leaned forward, imagining, for a brief moment, that this bleeding sailor, in his red jacket, might be the ghost of the other sailor, Thamus, who had long ago proclaimed my death. Thamus had finally come to apologize to me.

Then the sailor spoke again: "You called me *James*," he said. "You tried to hold my hand there by the river. To kiss me. I said you were mad, a strange little nymph. The river Eton, the place we used to go—remember how bright the sun was on those afternoons, Peter?"

I looked into the sailor's eyes.

He did not see me, but instead appeared to recall some long-ago moment.

"I pretend from time to time—" he said. "I pretend that—" He reached for me. "Come closer, Peter."

I crouched.

"Will you stroke my cheek," he said, "as you used to do?"

I touched him, ever so gently, with the sharp claw of my hand.

He raised his own bleeding stump. It appeared as though he thought he was stroking me as well.

"The ship came upon us swiftly," he whispered. "Pirates. Just off the coast of the island. What is the name of this island, Peter?"

Never-Was, I thought.

He sighed. "And my hand—my poor hand."

I gazed at the yellow shard of bone emerging from his wrist.

The sailor spread his lips. There was blood on his teeth. "So strange—" he said. "I dreamed of you just last night, Peter. We were together on board the ship, the *Roger*. Only, in my dream, it did not sail upon the waters. It *flew*. We travelled together through the clouds. I held you, and we watched a flock of gulls move around us like a school of silvery porpoises. When night fell, we did not land but glided still amongst the bright lamps of the stars."

I touched the sailor's cheek again. His flesh had turned cold.

"I wish that you would kiss me now," James said. "As once you wished to do."

I leaned forward. But before my lips touched his, I paused. Why I did, I cannot say. For wasn't this what I'd longed for? Wasn't this what I'd most desired? Yet to have it now, with a dying man—

It was in that pause that the sailor's eyelids fluttered. His eyes flashed bright. His gaze grew focused. And his expression changed. Fear passed over his dark features. He saw me for what I was. Not Peter. But the Goat. Not the boy he loved. But something he could not even imagine. Something that lived hidden away on an island. Something awful and sad.

The sailor's phantom hand fell away. His breath grew still.

Somewhere in the distance, I heard the divine voice speaking once again. *Pan is dead. And Peter is dead. And now so too, the captain.*

I lay down next to the dead man. I put my arms around him. We remained like that.

The sun set on the island, and the night birds began to sing.

THE MASS

Michel Vachey
translated from French by S. C. Delaney & Agnès Potier

According to all reports, the crowd isn't armed and moves with order and discipline. The wide band goes by at a constant speed. In front of an old-style electromagnet. Soon around ten thousand people. The number increases. Some students, workers come join those demonstrating. Work toward the back of the eye. Most are young people, boys and girls full of enthusiasm. They retain an ongoing image of vibrations. Among the crowd are soldiers in uniform. Base of the finger on the shaft. Stream of particles. Phosphorous. Sons of high officials having climaxed. Privileged position at the school. Between the labia minora. Reproduction of the image. The demonstrators carry land flags whose emblem has been removed. Until the end meets. Some signs carry the inscription: *Long live Earth's youth*. The track is erased within the unit. Moving back up, the fingertip grazes the shaft. At the end of the stroke it penetrates. Resonant signal. In principle, the demonstration is over. Many students, as expected, return in good order to their schools. Low current. Amplified before reaching the plateau. Some cracks thread the dark surface, revealing the incandescent matter underneath. Not all follow orders. The eye directed toward the dead eye. Pressure quite firm. It's not only students. The fluctuations around the head give rise to a variable field. No one new enters the scene. Band that unwinds before the folds. Gaping ring of flesh. The crowd inarticulate, anonymous, that won't disperse. By reversing things, the process is easy to imagine. When the wire falls under a variable field's influence, a current is generated in this wire. The crowd ebbs onto the bridges and moves in front of the Press Hall—flamboyant imitation of some French-Italian palace. Fingers absorbed to their tips, pressing, but not to the point of hurting.

It's there that the populations of all the districts converge. The dead eye. The effect is most pronounced when thread is wound round the lips. By 6 pm there are already 19,000 people, perhaps 24,000. The band moves on with its particles. Erasing measures. Reuse. The crowd vibrates, fraught with spasms. Sometimes the entire mass comes alive. Movement of the whole that radiates from the point of the seeming power source. Hardly anyone can hear what's being said, and it appears that nothing much is happening. The crowd asks that the egg that shines atop the Press Hall be extinguished. The band is neutralized. The balls, which are rare, small, and confined during periods of rest, swell, grow volatile, and multiply, spattering with yellow the surrounding skin that, with increasing rapidity, the flood engulfs and rends. The egg is turned off. Silver miniature. Broken in the trap. In the glass. Twice the square's light is cut off. Apparently to make people go home. Most remain. Given the running direction the head is placed on the left. The mouth positions itself atop the labia majora. The temperature rises, not only from the removal of the frozen film but also from the combustion of gases. Some people are rolling up newspapers which they set on fire and hold in the air like torches.

Corresponding volume settings. The input and output jacks are located in back or on the sides. It's nearly impossible to avoid contaminating the juvenile gases with the atmospheric air which circulates through the more or less porous, permeable layers. Repeatedly the crowd shouts. Tension maintained for one second. The previous evening it was decided that a proxy would stay on the premises to watch. Theoretically, all sources can be joined to the inputs. Without being grounded at once. Direct pollution. The proxy returns without having found anything. Short-lived flames of a lovely apple green. Near the apartment she runs into men armed with tommy guns and automatic pistols. Long exposures. Mouth connected to copper monochloride. Across 150 miles distance. Lights on in broad day-light in the villas. Effect of pressure against the top of the labia. For hours the crowd gathered in front of the hall. The distortions in the sound signal occur mainly at the level of the output transformer. It seems they've only asked the demonstrators to go home. Centered spray. Balls-and-sockets. Tip of the tongues. Joined after the output transformer.

FIVE POEMS

Daniel Owen

FOR REBEKAH SMITH

Sour tea for queens' resibilant air on done obscurities
and no fortune   Lost he visits desperate arts
at hours of sea and encinders a cigarette
like solipsistic wedding haze or locked queens experiencing
bro mass and peaking car ices   Sour tea
for these proletarian's nomads
that load ant totals with love

LATE SPERMATAZOA

Last nubile sea breeze fornicates. Lo obscure
saber, circle pallid dunes in the sky.
A sock vein decides a leaf undone
is the soul. The interior of last numbers
is anti absolute, a brilliant commotion of ache masses
crystallized. Care terrorizes cubicles
of Rama, holds jasmine and jade, hulled ass.
He permanently quiets the duration of the temporal
and hourly the reality of sea breeze swings.
Elfin violence and aristocratic groups of numbers
elope in distant directions.
Dustily I thank the heavens for having a lot of love
for the women for whom I care.
Dusty low obscurity, circling pallid obviousness
lost days come munching ache's communality.

THE SIRENS

Quiet the night sirens?
Yes.
The nebula cubes its door.
Parisian moans party.
The sirens signal lost corn lost gem ideas of nightlights.
The pro yawn of sequenced intentions desires me.
Salvage is the voice of your conscience.
My conscience paginates rote rock suicides.
An estimated night hour?
For your scripted yawn?
Crazy sin of importance.
Paperless posthumous, locating a permitted serenade radio?
Bastard.
It's a moveable hour.
A poor proportion absconds my pager.
Your page's heroin wronged a side of dental delay nightlights.
Conquering intended communication?
It's free.
It's song.
Indentured to many years of serene desertion
Like a high and low circle.

LAVE ANTENNAS

The patient legal ale of an extraneous city.
Site of eras of a mother, excuse ache dice in a soup
It's scalding. But no hay needle: it's Brooklyn and rice ass
of chaperones, delinquents, camels, pallid kids
of lost fruit bowl lines. My gut star arises, my gut star arises,
my gut star arises gently, dice and algae in concert with a century
of lemons. A period of apnea's lost couch.

Lame yuck action became a mirror for the lave antenna
of a hotel. Oh forget deep alabaster, an imaginary Brooklyn
mediates night on the street, the gentle tease happy
the novel, the stars like gems encrusted
in a book of extraneous never terminating day leer
(ailments of this earth), the night, the sea,
gently happy this a-somatic fauna vents an aberration.

All the sadness of its toy years
seeps toward continuance.

TR-ANQ-UIL

When the lagoon has a force of deserved lame adoration
that seeds transformation in the flower in the obscured
of your corpse, the cased seer of lost eyes
powders sentience's tired May hour the cold of gargantua
that city of free ice like a donated constant,
the plume that hastens causal quizzes, the flocked hours
accedeicide hastens, a single lock that inobstinately
returns its night of your Delhi of pure tea
cold giants and sun rises reunite capacious day
with the dispersed fragments of the ruin:
its extreme elegance has recharged a zealot's door
problematizingly seeing your nerves, your sadness,
the stomach that you cruel in the center of
all aesthetics keen to hasten the projection
the sunrise perdition has encased in a sigil
and the pale look of courts and doors, a lisp seeps pillows and the eTryes'
azure profundities go crazy and good and
can't reveal our others

FOUR POEMS

Alexis Pope

Bobby Briggs

that ex whose ringtone was *killing me softly*

strumming my pain with

blessed be the weak for

I'm left with a storm in my chest

dark, heavy cloud

what it feels like to be her

the young girl

I have not forgotten

armageddon of being left

door behind me I cracked you

nothing to bite on for security's sake

little soft lake to my left

somewhere the ringer is

playing and I'm sleeping in christie's bed

reaching over her

to silence my phone

cold drunken face

my legs around

nothing you felt was real

just another tumble from the roof

another punctured lung

I swore you would die, mr.

I almost prayed that you might

land next to me the next time

your body was found in the low-cut grass

the tree branch an arrow

by which I might cast the next spell

love my dearly you

become me

underwater in a recently shocked pool

Day 1

Under the house the limes grow. A train rattles over our heads. It seems we are always living below something or otherwise. A bell and then lowering. A fresh bowl of water.

Some days feel shorter than the others so we walk to the beach. The time Carrie was a cat and my mother laughed so hard. She can't turn it off though. I tell her about some good medications. We don't talk about sex.

Sleep collides with wake and he makes biscuits in the morning. Mishears "Maine" as "mine." *I thought you had a new accent.*

No, the blueberries, I say.

The underpants say Monday which is correct. Although not yesterday, she smacks my butt and puts a tongue in my mouth. I didn't know the mail worked on Labor Day.

Deliveries for a birthday. Clay on small hands. I hope to never move from this moment, I think as it passes.

Morning Poem

Which morning is this
A cicada begins
Walk the dog and dream about it
Wife is just another word
If she were
There has to be a way
Like cat hair
I cover my glass
For protection
A way to say it correct
A poem is a wall
Or the reverse
I build myself a new one
Each morning before
Amethyst
Like honey
The children
Smell ripe
For what do I wet my lips
Cardboard box
Wheels on a cart on a sidewalk
Crinkling plastic bag
Those girls make good receptacles
My mom told me a good lot
She's had work done

Like what a spider does
With her legs
The creators rather
It's not playing god
One nation under
Language
How much force
To push a stroller
Always pushing or being
It's a feeling
To center an object
To call it one's own
Or is it a bridge
For the other to walk across
I'll be that
If she gets to the other side
I'm breaking
This apart
It's not jogging
If you're trying to make the train
That's the thing with time
Always so much or
The reverse
Green and yellow morning
We were arguing about a mascot
What defines
We have to understand
The root of the tree
Man on the podcast explains
How best to eat worms
Garlic
It's so obvious
What the training wheels do
Trust exercise
What even is help

Or language
This breaking the creation
Walk the dog again to dream
Don't stress about it
Smile you're on candid
A cicada if she were
None of this should happen
A wall to crash into
I'm at the center
Breaking the bread apart
Rolling
My tongue over the language
Or down the grass
Arms over chest
Eyes closed so tight
It's not spinning but
About discovery
What even is
A description
Like a street sign
Simplicity
A plastic bag
Clipping a cat's nails
That's the trouble
History
Doesn't change until we
Grow to be a part of it

Another Degree

I take on the snow
To remove it   who asks the right
Questions a verdict which comes in
Freezing
to the bone
        but we manage
To heat through
To cut
I become remains
  To signify the problem
To let it overcome
    What engulfs
: the question of remains
I don't matter
To lay hands on   with holy water
Wash them
        By lowering into the well
Of sadness what do you mean
  And how do you consume it
When woken from sleep
Generously with butter and salt
What noise escapes you
One looks in the mirror for
    Generous containment
The problem of the day

And how do you manage
  Inside on
Your accounts deepen
The black kind of blue
  Dirty with your poor
The pockets licked clean
  I have chosen my debts
And well
Frozen *to the bone*
To bleach is an absence of
What I bathe in
   But mine is a home
The invoice to prove
The payments I can't make
  What is the out
When we're so enclosed with
The deep side of the pool
Called a diver
  Or runner at the very
No news of late
Another degree removes
  What I've never
The water in me
What we can't drown

FIVE POEMS

Andrew Cantrell

Year Zero

What will we do the first year? We'll mob beginnings. We'll mask blank ritual objects like we said. By touch beggared and carefully young and only by touch thrown-in and numb as a glimmer in any sentimental replica will we bind colors to objects and objects to themselves. This will absorb entirely the obstinate attachment of things to measure.

Yes and the second year we'll detach things from discourse. We'll spring from measure the rustle of silver wheat in moonlight. The terrors born of every murmured voice and every metered stroke. Meted by the agonies of an era we'll detourn the details of a distance in the ebb of objects in themselves. Therefore no true disclosure nor any true coming-forth unless we attain readymade to the faction of our speaking.

Afterwards in the sleety cough of the weathers of the third year we'll discern the marred protocols in rasping winter-time alleys of things attached to things. Of us to each other. Of any objects altogether. Accordingly entire civil architectures will acquire aurorae as immanent as any and in every color whatsoever. We'll designate therefore always manifold beginnings.

An end is a term the hand searches for

The exile's role is serious itself   It's to hold (in) dimmed the diminishing
sky of a late looking-out on last treetops   of a journey in silver rustle of
a rattling rail car

and a flight snared in the asphalt vanishings and barricades   of the stage
or street   It's to hold   in this lifting of slowly applied layers   overlain
on lost streets

Thus does each sound and each moment come to turn   and falteringly
mount to the other

How problems of migration direct opposites   in vases   bowls   plates
and boxes   where thinking suddenly stops in a part   and is laden with
every ghosting voice and other's trimming

Their force spent in past appraisals makes me similar to dwelling-places
furniture and   clothes

How   fugitive   our arts divulged the manufactory gauge   generalized
the terrors born of bread-less weeks

How instrumental idols spared industry made clockwork in articulated
lines   the howling factory of the present gone monstrous against insurgent

futures

How over-determining every stroke of a pleased philanthropy   they
cease to understand our longing

But we do not cease to understand it

Skyward this storm   measured to its end   meted by the agonies of an
early exile   My hand can still dream of a brush   violently   against the
grain

A chorus is somehow

That which is communication   *I hope I make enough tonight*   is in an instant   from the secrecy of work   *so that I never have to   work again*

Is instinctively   from the secrecy in every conversation   that which place fixes   in letters and words   in their susurant murmurings   so faintly impressed   to the earth's surface

How it in its distant knowing instant   How diffident   you lift your arm as   diffident   I extend my hand   How a mirror retains   How a mirror remains

How there is no speaking   without the murmur of the world   where our positions are different   Not only in this   or only by this   entering into the tractor-trailer cab

Diffident as an effort   I can only hope to return   place returns

When I descended   *Hell is Real*   into clouds   *caused by light other than that forming the image*   hounded from and to any new skyline at all   from the Cumberland Plateau

Adults Only   Sunny and cloudless at 7 am   distant and relaxed   *diffused*

by the substance that caused it   I thought   *Today I'll see better*

So descending into clouds   half storm half fog   I didn't know if we
were apart   *A sick call was required*   if it was a part of another   one other
tractor trailer   that had burned that morning

North and west of Nickajack lake   or a car that had been struck

There were just some letters and some words   from the noise that is
internal

A chorus is somehow   a place that can somehow   direct us   to recognize
the object perceived   a place that somehow   directs human wounding

You making money tonight?   It is a repetition   elapsed as the talking   *Not
much*   of an   of always an   outsider

It is the murmur of sense   that always makes of sense   of the surfaces
of our murmuring   an effort to voice resonance

They are   we are   here   each of us   images   each caused by light other
than that forming the images   of our positions   or movements

The last hour of the longest day

How much was promised   in driving inclemencies   by the thoughts that
were developing here   in rain drops dead   in black amaranth

How much after all were we owed   domain of a moment's dark dwelling
by this dream of redemption   that was by nature not obliging

How many times in the night   olive in light of street-lamp's shadowed
jumble   did I repeat the mad hourly requiring   rain slick in limbs of
newly budded elms   that a question be set in motion

How morning would set us down   in hew of lacustrine cloud   out of
a sensation of terror   hued lavender and black   freezing in the air   of
the question's behest

How we would in this undertaking   dire designees of the past's immediate
deriving   in this motion and immensity   as-yet-un-fated   admit of a
wild disorder

How justice does not await an argument

How little patches of color shine   where despite myself I dwelt the day
through the fresh exploitation of the proletariat   dire in human chorus

How namely by that form and that content   substance the reluctant
factory of social policy   we found our present and our selves   essence
the civil architecture of uncivil worlds

How bad infinity becomes a tactical arm of desire   an untoward unjoining
and a strip of light under bedroom doors   by which they sell austerity
with special pleading

How this violence   its lexicon of wasp nests   nonetheless   and
superstructures' first uneven accumulation of us   continually from past
and possible   limbs   the rains haven't wet yet   may

Excavate   sedimentary   our antagonisms   unnumbered because
innumerable   in courtyards and in which a lamp is burning

How in genuine sorrow   estuarine gulls a-skim lakeside wastes of air
and in anger abhorred   hesitant between opposite and system   we may
linger a bit   haunted by this

How chilled by rain's desultory advent   dead in black amaranth   how
much was promised   and how much disguised   by this moment   a found
scission   unlooked-for   of the longest day   of its storm and wreckage

How we yet bear forth   as-yet-un-fated points of intensity   yet   how
How the layers of the present seem to cover us   yet   how

S e a r o a r

We accrete ourselves as wasp or orchid to our own dismantling   An
orchid presses two glints   glint of a wasp or orchid's trembling gist

A wasp is not only a wasp   A wasp is before   It's the line of a moment
that's more   of a movement that's an and   and an or   and an orchid
presses itself by or as a word   as a moon

as what is seen   as an and that arcs to be at the first   at the roaring word
of our roaring worlds   as sea-roar a-soar on one wave or more   wan and
worn   line of a movement   bay of a moment

or more   oared by blank words only   from which an emptiness pours
onto which a blank world would mirror a soaring word   a cousinship out
of language

Twined around a world an orchid presses a-roar   for a movement or
what's more for a moment before   out of which coppery glints a wasp
becoming in its a-parallel on-coming

a becoming-more that presses us   presages us   a visage of an orchid in
copper as the glint of a visible word   as viscid we accrete to an orchid or

another's roar in the pour of a wasp's and

and even-and-more   such is the blank world we accrete as a wasp or an
orchid or an or   as copper   an orchid glints   or what's more the or of
a wasp or a word and so soars   an accretion

borne by the lure of the narrows of a sorrow that it designates   as a word
or a world   a sign or a signal of an inaccessible face

A-roar in the soar of surer moons   where only the word or the world is
a subject   and only of an inaccessible place   we soar past the point of
accession to the more of an inaccessible face

to its labyrinth   where we wander sure as a word of an ever-more   our
accretion a-glint well past the other's word   a blank word mirrored wanly
by a roar as by a moon   of which we may

speak   a blank world hurled roaring forth from the sorrows of its soaring
and belated aurorae

and where surging we accrete even and more to another's or another
word of a world

our a-parallel becoming a coming to something   as turning we accrete
to a pouring-forth of an originary emptiness   as returning we ask what
another's roar requires of us   when to that

emptiness both roar and other are subject   only as a moment or at most
almost as a movement   a humming as we accrete in copper glints to a
world or a word and only to a word or a world

for which a wasp roars   (for) which an orchid presses by signifying   a becoming that's a to-be or at least an ardor to be an occasion of a coming-before

So we are pressed   pressed nevertheless   presaged and expressed in time as a sign that soars out in hurrying fines from our swerving lines   to which copper glints that heave toward

absolutely nothing have accreted   an absolutely something else

So another's roar's an a-parallel more of a signifying or   so an orchid presses us   presages us   as a wasp or a word   an if-only or a more   of a common and coming world   of copper glints

thrown from before   so we pass so signifying from this labyrinth   a surge out of a language that's external   where there's an and to an any and a then to an and that's eternal

So we're accreted by our dismantling to a wasp and a word and an other's roar   to an orchid and a world all wafted awash from an emptiness   out of which courses a line of a flagging world's

trembling gists   wan in the beginnings of a coppery sea   out of which glints the sure and soaring furrows of an and and an even-more   that's beyond measure

AS WE TALKED, OTHER MUTANTS BEGAN TO APPEAR

Susan Daitch

1.

The Art of War

Soldiers in World War I etched designs and cartoon-like figures into discarded artillery shell casings about fourteen inches high, two inches in diameter. Here's Little Nemo in Slumberland, the Katzenjammer Kids, Gertie the Dinosaur, animated just before war broke out. The soldiers were so young, and comics were the last toehold of civilian life. For the time it took to engrave the casings and for the seconds it took to enjoy the pictures, the war slows down, or is suspended, not for as long as the Christmas truce, and not throughout the whole network of the trenches, but for a few minutes, for a few feet.

The Tlingit decorated their armor with Chinese coins and puffin beaks. The coins date from 1644–1796, years which mark the reigns of four successive Chinese emperors. It was, for the Tlingit trading with Siberians, a more practical use for Chinese currency. The armor protected from more than bullets. It was also thought to protect from spirits that would infect and take over. Thousands of miles to the south, warriors from the Kirábati Islands wore helmets made from puffer fish, also known as the porcupine fish. They look like pale globes studded with spikes. The tribesmen used the materials at hand, just as iron from meteorites was used for making daggers by the Tuareg in north Africa, just as, hundreds of years later, the border fence between the United States and Mexico is made out of recycled helipads from the Vietnam and Korean wars. Subterranean oil molecules turn into plastic, interstellar atoms of iron end up piercing terrestrial bodies; reincarnation takes many forms.

On the shores of Kiràbati, hundreds of green plastic bottles washed up on a shore huddled around rocks look like a photomicrograph of a cluster of viruses or bacteria attacking cells. What use the seafaring plastic bottles can be put to remains to be seen.

2.

The Raven and the Messenger

In 1935 anthropologist Frederica de Laguna traveled to Alaska to record the stories and culture of the Tlingit, the Dena, and other tribes. Her memoir described such circumstances as not being able to write a personal check for camping equipment at a Philadelphia Sears and Roebuck because Roosevelt had closed the banks for a day, but meanwhile, the clock was ticking. She had to catch a train, a boat, a bush plane. As it would turn out, all the camping and other equipment she and her crew so desperately needed only arrived minutes before their boat was to depart for the Alaskan interior. In 1935, she was one of the very few women explorers to venture into remote and dangerous parts of the world where travel entailed risk and awe. Accurate maps, alidades, and compasses could be a matter of life or death.

The only maps available at that time were from earlier United States Geological Survey reconnaissance teams, but even the rivers and settlements marked on them may not have been as precise as she hoped. Some of the maps she referenced had been drawn as early as 1842. She also used census reports to determine who was where, and *The Handbook of American Indians North of Mexico*, the 1910 edition, which mapped "every tribe, village, or band, but its entries were so brief or confused it was of little practical use." The handbook, meant to be a guide, contained not only sparse but contradictory information. Along with these imperfect documents de Laguna included reports by a man named Ivan Petroff, though his writings, based on documents reported to be translated from Russian, turned out to be forgeries. Petroff didn't go as far into the Yukon as he claimed, though he stated the native tribes were "treacherous and warlike." She did the best she could with what she had.

Operating on a shoestring, for this was the height of the Depression, we launched at Nenana two skiffs of our own making and unconventional design, like the most foolhardy party that ever embarked on the great river. For the next eighty days, over a distance of 1,600 miles, we fared through what was then truly a wilderness, looking for ancient archeological sites and recording our adventures and misadventures, our many disappointments and few lucky finds, and above all, our rewarding contacts with the Native peoples and white people we met along the way.

She was far from the first to make contact with native tribes. The Spanish had made as far north as Nootka Sound; English, Koreans, and Russians had traded with indigenous peoples for centuries. The Russian-American Company paid for shells and furs in rubles. Money was more useful for the metal it contained than as currency, and so often coins were melted down to be put to other uses. Iron, rare and strongest of all, reached them via shipwrecks and was called drift iron. Knives made from drift iron were referred to as ghosts of angry men.

By the time de Laguna arrived, she observed, "guns, steel traps, and steel snares took the place of deadfalls, stone-headed hunting spears, bows and arrows." Hunting large animals like bears had previously been a group effort: a hunter with a spear backed up by archers. With the introduction of firearms, this became not only a solitary activity, but no longer only the province of men. Women could hunt, become self-sufficient, manage dog teams, survive in the wild, support herself and her family.

In villages up the coast de Laguna described masks, totem poles, carvings of sharks, wolves, and bears guarding houses or ornamenting lintels, posts. She encountered shamans wearing conical hats decorated by sea lion whiskers and nose rings made of copper, silver, or iron. There were taboos regarding bears and women, sharks shouldn't be hit on the head, eyes were painted on bird wings so they would know where and how to fly. What did these representations mean to the inhabitants? Terror or awe? Honor or horror? Her informants, even in 1935, made her feel that the definitive answer may have already been lost, or altered so much from some original story as to be unrecognizable. She recorded Raven stories which proliferated among the tribes on both sides of the Bering Sea. The Tlingit's stories were the most organized, and in them the Raven, like the anthropomorphic characters of many myths, displayed avian abilities and human traits. He was a trickster, fond of duping men and animals alike. In creation stories, Raven formed men from pinecones. Their war-like tendencies would distract from his tricks.

When de Laguna returned to the region thirty years later, she observed that dog teams had been replaced by snowmobiles, and the new technology brought perhaps as many drawbacks as advantages. If the snowmobile broke down far from any human habitation, the driver could become stranded with no hope of rescue. Dogs can sense thin ice; the machine cannot. If dogs misjudge, and the front of the team does fall through ice, they can be rescued. A snowmobile and driver just fall through and are never seen again. Though it was not yet true during the years of de Laguna's visits to the Arctic, global warming now makes the hazards of falling through thin ice even more likely and treacherous.

The ice is truly crystalline, but even as far away as the Yukon, grains of plastic from bottles can be found embedded in it. The bottles from trash dumps, cruise ships, spillage from cargo containers fallen overboard drift north on ocean streams, and even though the original plastic shape has been degraded beyond recognition, identifiable particles can be found in the ice. They are plentiful.

3.

Watery

If you had x-ray vision on the subway one of the things you might see, apart from skeletons seated and standing, are hundreds of little clear plastic containers of Purell hidden in bags and pockets. The scant few ounces of disinfectant are held in a bottle faceted to appear not just liquid but also crystalline. The label promises to kill germs like nothing else.

The gel is packaged to signify purity and cleanliness, though it's actually neither of these. There are warnings, not on the bottles but commonly found elsewhere, which predict the overuse of antibacterial agents will lead to the ultimate resistance on the part of the microbes. The disinfectant meant to be so toxic to their one-celled bodies will be rendered neutral by its ubiquity. Future generations of germs will be like super heroes or super bugs. They will prosper and wreak havoc in the face of the water-like, but not water, gels designed to annihilate them. The microbes run amok. They win.

But until that moment when armed and defended microbes are victorious, the anti-bacterials provide a border. To the microbes, the film of Purell constitutes a fence, electrified and lethal, but like most fences, it has its limits and can be circumnavigated. They might bang what passes for their heads against it: you let in degrading plastic and all kinds of chemical agents! Why not us! We have our benefits. How shortsighted to leave us out!

4.

The Orange Jumpsuits

Where are they made? China? Mexico? The secrets in the factory's order files must be legion. On the other end, it's someone's job to place the orders for the orange jumpsuits. There are parts of the world in which delivery of goods isn't easy, and the solutions to this problem could be the stuff of bad stand up, like 50s era, take my wife jokes. I don't want to make light of the seriousness of what happens to the people who are made to wear the orange jumpsuits, but like following the money, I'm interested in following the small details, the grommets and wing-nuts of how people do what they do, even when it is the unspeakable, but without wanting to cloak the unspeakable in the banality of the support structure that makes the unspeakable possible. The orange jumpsuits are sent and delivered to prisons known and unknown, the Black Sites, but also to locations remote and dangerous, and if it is difficult to get deliveries to these parts of the world, though they can acquire a variety of armaments, perhaps the orange jumpsuits are washed and reused.

5.

Martians Just Like Us

In *Martian Infiltration*, a comic by Al Feldstein published in 1950, Martians have infiltrated the Defense Department. They look, sound, and dress exactly like Americans in positions of power, but the Secretary of State has his suspicions. With the help of an unnamed but handsome blond assistant, the pair determine that there is a sub-group, a fraternity within the Defense Department, whose membership is Martian-only. How to determine who among them is from Mars and who isn't? The Secretary of State knows that visitors from the Red Planet don't reflect infrared light, and therefore, when photographed, their physical bodies will be invisible.

In order to prove membership is strictly alien, the assistant stations himself in a small room across the street from a building they believe is the clubhouse for the secret group. For an entire day he takes pictures with a camera loaded with infrared film. Sure enough, when the pictures are developed and printed, walking uniforms, bodies invisible, are seen entering and leaving the club. Admirals, generals, colonels, majors, Martians; all and all masquerading as trusted Americans in positions of power and authority. Caps perched on the space where a head would be—all invisible heads smoking cigarettes, cigars, a pipe. One holds a lighter.

Knowing they'll be in the clubhouse at a particular hour, the Secretary of State hatches a plan to annihilate all of the take-over artists, but in order to control public opinion, their eradication must look like an accident. (The word terrorism had not yet come into common parlance.) A Dr. Bergson is summoned. Not a Martian, though he has Op Art eyes, the scientist gives them a vial of deadly bacteria, instructing them to uncork it in such a way that its contents will be wafted throughout the building by the air conditioning system. Since his concoction is resistant to any anti-bacterial agent, inhalation of the microbes is fatal.

The two heroes arrive at the Defense Department Club at 8:00 in the evening, but their plans don't go as smoothly as they'd hoped. Captured and taken to the throne room, they receive an unspeakable shock. Flanked by General MacArnold and Admiral Kingsley is the Secretary of Defense! Full of confidence, he describes how Martians infiltrated the American government at its highest levels. It was easy pickings. There is no diabolical laugh indicated here, but the expression on the Martian leader's face is one of glee and delight. But not for long—it's later than he thinks. The deadly potion has already begun to do its work. The Secretary of State reveals that he and his assistant aren't Earthlings at all but survivors of Martian tyranny on Venus. They will die on this night, too, but at least for the moment they've halted the Martian takeover of the United States. From his death bed the handsome Venusian warns Americans that the alien invaders are only temporarily thwarted. They will be back...

In other Feldstein comics, Martians and space aliens are portrayed with eye stems, insect legs, tentacles with swollen suction cups, or sentient brains suspended in jars, but in *Martian Infiltration*, their true selves are just like us, completely humanoid except when photographed with infrared film. Feldstein wrote over five hundred comic scripts, horror and science fiction, but the real terror, he believed, was nuclear proliferation, and he lamented the fact "we are all armed to the teeth." In 1953 artist Marie Severin drew a caricature of Al Feldstein at his drawing board reading Mickey Spillane. A copy of *McCarthy and You* lies on the floor a few feet away.

6.

Major Byron

Also known as Monsieur Memoir, George Gordon de Luna Byron claimed that his father was Lord Byron and his mother was a Spanish countess, the Countess de Luna of Cadiz. He got his title, he maintained, while employed by the East India Company, but at the time he was presenting this version of himself, he had never enlisted in any army or fought in any wars. His scams were numerous and clever, as if one day while sitting in his house in Wilkes Barre, Pennsylvania, he assessed what he did have and figured out how to turn his talents into cash. He would often don the uniform of a British soldier, though where and how he acquired his titles, rank, and the decorations that supported them was unknown. His fictitious military exploits included the command of a regiment of sepoys in India. In the middle of the nineteenth century, as now, anyone could stake a claim to or steal the identity of Citizen X. But in the Major's time, ways of proving who was who could be cumbersome. Eyewitness or documentary evidence that would contradict a claim would take time to find and disseminate, and even then not everyone would get the news. Monsieur Memoir had an advantage in that Byron was dead. He wasn't talking.

The Major wrote to Lord Byron's publisher, John Murray, making a claim on the poet's estate, and although John Murray pretty much told him to get lost, undeterred, Byron II wrote to his father's friends asking if they would lend him their personal letters for a biography he was writing. Believing him to be a long lost son, they complied, and so in this way, he got his hands on the original letters of Shelley and Keats. Making careful study of their handwriting, he was able to ink copies that were so convincing he sold them with little trouble, and made a bundle. He used turquoise ink, blue-grey paper artificially aged and speckled. In the letters he complained of physical ailments including lameness and the endemic sorrows of poets in England. The handwriting was so assured, no quavering or unsteadiness, that even publishers were deceived, but eventually suspicion about the flood of Byron documents interfered with sales. The ranks of the gullible dried up, and he returned stateside, though duping Americans turned out not to be as easy as he projected. An editorial in *The New York Daily Mirror* described him in not just unflattering terms, but let any cat he thought might be in the bag altogether out.

The first glance at his person gave us an instinctive conviction that both himself and his "inedited works" were a sham; and we turned from him with the natural disgust we feel for humbugs in general, and literary humbugs in particular.

He responded.

The same secret influence that was active against me in London, is now behind the scenes in New York. I know the Agent of Murray, who has slandered me... but shortly, the instant when the trial of the 'Evening Mirror' comes on, I shall have it in my power to unmask the man — no — reptile. Lord Byron, though accused of the foulest crimes at one period — never defended himself — I have adopted the same tactics — my answer to the unscrupulous malignity of the fastidious gentry of the press is silence and contempt.

Some of the texts he made up himself, but reproducing portions of the letters that already existed in print was one of the mistakes that led to his detection in 1852. Using another one of his pseudonyms, De Gliber, the Major attempted to sell a Byron manuscript, but the forger penned his work on paper bearing a 1834 watermark, ten years after the poet's death. Despite sloppiness and copying what already existed, the Byron hoax remained successful for nearly a decade; so successful that many of his forgeries can be found in the British Library. Some were even sold to John Murray of Abelmarle Street himself, as well as to Mary Shelley.

Despite his grand history including a scam that involved gold mines in Mexico, Major Byron's only actual military experience was as a forty-four-year-old private in the Fifth New Jersey Light Artillery during the Civil War. His days as Major Byron of London and Paris were behind him. He spent much of the Civil War in a hospital, claiming paralysis, though at the end of the war, he walked out of the ward in fine shape. When he died in 1882, his obituary read:

He posed at various times as a litterateur, a journalist, a diplomatist, a government agent, an officer of the British Army in the East Indies, a British naval officer, an officer of the United States Army, a mining prospector, a broker, a merchant, a spy, an agent for cotton claims, a commission agent, an Oriental traveler, a representative of European mercantile interests, a bookseller, a patent rights agent, a gentleman of means, and an aristocratic exile, expatriated and pensioned on condition that he should never reveal his genealogy.

7.

Orange is the New Mouse

Meanwhile, in a lab in Santa Cruz, a biologist with an interest in creating hardier fruit inserted a mouse gene into the DNA of an orange, so that the fruit would be resistant to both blight and frost. To a strand of RNA, a blastocyst is a cotton candy-shaped nebulae. The orange looks and tastes like an orange, but somewhere inside you wonder if there is potential for a future generation of oranges grown from these seeds to form fruit which, though round and citrusy in every way, sprout little furry mouse ears, and maybe even a tail. The embryonic Byronic copy that fools some, but really bears no relation to Byron, yet can try on any number of identities till the original is lost from sight.

FATHERS AND SONS

Gabriel Blackwell

I did not find my father at home when I returned. My sister said he was gone. I think we must have played in her room until dinner was ready. I do not remember what we had for dinner that night. I read this in the letter and wonder: Can one write—is it even *possible* to write—about the disappearance of one's father the way one would write about, for instance, stamp collecting, I mean when it's someone else who has done the collecting? Is it possible, I guess is what I'm asking, to write about one's father's disappearance as though the fact of his having gone missing were just something that other people are, maybe even somewhat inexplicably, intrigued by, but which seems more or less completely uninteresting to oneself? I suppose the answer must be yes.

And, look, before we go any further, please understand, I am a miserable person and I know it. My good fortune has, for instance, never seemed particularly good to me. I have, on an embarrassing number of occasions, only just barely stopped myself from complaining about the problems my wife and I have with our son to someone who, for all I know, can't have kids, or lost one young. There are those who have it worse, I mean, and, in my better moments, I recognize that my way of seeing the world is cowardly and childish and to be regretted. And there is also the convenient deafness I tend to develop when my daughter demands my attention, and the reproach I see in my son's face when I tell him I love him—though of course I know there is no reproach there, not really— and then there is also my tendency to make things about me when, in fact, they aren't.

My trip to the library was, then, as I saw it, a duty, an obligation I felt I owed my father. It was my father who wrote this letter, about *his* father, my grandfather, and I guess I couldn't stand to see my father's words seem uncaring by comparison. I needed, I mean, to compare. I did not want my father to be alone. So I trailed along behind the librarian, not dawdling exactly, not drawing things out, only being careful not to get too close to this woman, a woman who, frankly, to me, had seemed to cultivate the distance I was trying to keep through her bearing and also through her attitude, a woman appearing, at first, physically frail but carrying herself as though she in fact possessed a wild strength—a woman, that is, depressingly familiar in her affect (familiar, I mean, to me), but also, it seemed, a sincerely helpful and solicitous person, even if very possibly, I thought, incapable of showing it—this librarian, then, handing me any number of books, mysteries, yes, thrillers, true crime, all books dealing with the sudden disappearances of both men and women, handing me book after book so that the pile rose to my chin, and then, finally, a book clad in plain binding on which I could not find a title, saying, *This one may interest you*, her strange, possibly unintentional emphasis on the word *you* and the lack of a title on the book somehow together sparking a memory in me, a memory from two or three years earlier, when I'd been in this same library, this time with my son, handing him impossibly thick books, books without illustrations, all of them about birds, thinking perhaps *this* will be the one that finally bores him as much as the whole subject bores me, perhaps *this* one will cure him—and I knew, even back then, that I was being ridiculous, even insensitive, insulting, stupid—cure him, that is, of this fascination, this obsession so that, for once, he and I could have a normal conversation, one in which both of us participated and responded to each other, one in which I did not feel as though I was interviewing him for *Birding Enthusiasts Monthly*, one that I wouldn't complain about later, in bed, to my wife, so that, turning out the light with a heavy sigh, she wouldn't look at me as though seeing someone she didn't recognize and say, *Would it kill you to take an interest? He's reaching out, as much as he can.*

I looked again at the book—at the book*s*, plural—the librarian had handed me. I thought, surely, if I looked close enough, in each one there would be some near-explanation or partial excuse for my father's tone, some hidden wrinkle to his story. Then I thought of the weight of these books in my hands and the flat affect of the librarian and I worried that I was really only corralling yet more facts, crowding out the finer feelings I'd hoped to uncover, and so, saddened, I could think only of leaving the library. As soon as the librarian had passed out of the line of my sight, I left the books on the cart I found at the end of the aisle and slunk away, knowing, as the books slid out of my hands, that the librarian would later find this stack, arranged in the reverse order she had handed the books to me, on the cart, and in that moment know that, though she'd done her best, I had nonetheless failed to follow through, failed to hold up my end of the bargain, failed to so much as consider her efforts—know, in other words, that I was, quite simply, not a serious person, not someone to be trusted. Perhaps, like my son—and, like my son, innocent of such motivation—she would then shield herself further from those who did not share her enthusiasms by learning even more about those enthusiasms. Perhaps she would be as bewildered as my son was to find that common ground had become even scarcer in the process. Who cared for her? Who listened patiently? I didn't know.

I'm not likely to come off well in this, I know, but I still feel as though I should say my actions were not, whatever they might seem, the result of some wanton cruelty. I had already read quite a few stories of disappearances, including even one or two of the ones the librarian had handed me. I knew the general tenor, I'm saying. I had a sense of the literature. *That* wasn't my problem. Though its effects had been hidden from me at the time, this reading had, in the end, succeeded really only in making me more anxious: here were stories, above all, of men and women for whom life had simply become too much, though often this part of the story was buried beneath the testimony of those who'd known them. *He seemed so happy*, they wrote. *Life was good. He had so much to look forward to.* Yes, all had seemed perfectly normal to everyone around these people, much as my own life seemed then to me, before, I guessed, I'd begun reading, but then, inexplicably, they went missing. There were, invariably, questions: Had there been secret debts? A second family? A fatal diagnosis? Perhaps it was only among the families of the missing, but it really started to seem as though every man, woman, and child harbored the same exact suspicion, that there had to be something someone out there was not telling them. One Saturday, not long ago, my wife told me, a propos of nothing, *You know he loves you*, and I immediately thought, to my great shame, *Why is she telling me this? Did he do something I don't know about? Will I hear something from his aide on Monday?* I was, I mean, not exempt. Far from it.

My father's name, my father had written, *is or was Rudolph Fentz*. See? Only the first line and already I had a question: Why *is or was?* Really, though, I had many questions. I had, first of all, no idea why my father was writing this to me, and then, I hadn't known Rudolph Fentz, had been born much too late to have met him, hadn't even known his story. I had, as a child, often been compared to him, especially in terms of our temperaments, and I felt then that these comparisons must have been unfavorable, though perhaps they only *seemed* unfavorable because Rudolph Fentz was a man I'd never met, the comparisons, then, coming off as though I were being judged to be an unknown, an unknowable, even, a phantasm, something one could not say was definitively one thing or another, good or bad, liked or merely tolerated, but, then again, perhaps my father saw something in me, some dormant, suspect gene he had, unwittingly, passed on and of which he was, in his own way, trying to warn me.

In any case, most of what I knew of my grandfather came by way of these comparisons. To go by what my father said, I shared not only my grandfather's features but also some of his mannerisms, the same inscrutability, the same uncertain bearing, the same nervous energy. Was my father, in those moments, willing me to display some atavistic relationship to his father? Is the saying really *The son is the father of the man*, or is that some Freudian thing my mind is doing to me? Not that my father ever treated me as his father, but it did seem, in reading the letter, as though I were reading a story that was making obscure promises to reveal some deeper aspect of our relationship.

And despite the letter's ostensible subject, there isn't much about Rudolph Fentz there. My father sticks to the facts, and so, because there are so few facts about his father's disappearance, there simply isn't much to the letter. It is, in total, two pages, hand-written, front and back. Somehow, the letter's thinness makes it seem as though Rudolph Fentz was merely one of many fathers who disappeared during my father's childhood. My father's feelings seem to be concentrated in this one line, a non sequitur: *I remember I did not like it when he kissed me because his beard scratched my skin.* That single sentence made me realize that, in relating only the events that occurred rather than how he felt about those events, my father was actually avoiding the story he'd set out to tell. I did not know whether he knew this.

Though I had a beard when my son was born, I have since shaved it. I can remember him fussing and crying after I'd kissed him on the top of his head, the radiant look of anger he would get seemingly any time I got near, and my wife's reaction, especially after she'd put him down. The first few times, I figured it was me and just felt embarrassed, but, with repetition, my embarrassment was replaced by a dull kind of anger. Why did he react this way to me? To me, I mean, and not to, say, my wife or my mother-in-law?

Because, I suppose, my father had been hospitalized when my grand-father disappeared, and because he'd been terribly ill even before that, where one might expect a matter-of-fact report on my grandfather's last hours at home, there is, in the letter, nothing. My father did not, could not, know what those hours were like, and perhaps it did not occur to him to wonder, so he's substituted a brief paragraph on what was known of his illness at the time he was hospitalized. It seemed there were many misconceptions going around then, about, most perniciously, the severity and the spread of the disease, but also about its causes and its prognoses. Rudolph Fentz in particular had, apparently, been warned that, because of certain personal risk factors out of his control, he was not only susceptible to the disease but even likely to develop a fatal case should he contract it. He had therefore been counseled to stay far away from the hospital. It could only have been torment for him, one supposes.

It hardly seems necessary to say that his son, my father, was terribly sick, in fact, on the verge of death at this time, and Ingrid Fentz, Rudolph's wife, my grandmother, was at the hospital nearly around the clock, sleep-ing on a rickety steel cot the staff had brought in for her, and eating only on the rare occasions some nurse remembered to put an extra plate on the tray. She would later say she felt sorry for Rudolph Fentz—it was *his* son, after all, that he couldn't see—but at the time she must also have felt deeply angry with him for not visiting, not helping out, and, because she hadn't slept much and had eaten even less, her nerves, at that time, must have been frazzled. Now, it's true I've made up some of these details, maybe even most of them, but please understand I did it only because it seemed necessary. No one else is going to bother to do it. Anyway, it's basically clear from the letter's subtext that Ingrid and Rudolph fought over who ought to be at the hospital, that one of them must have been there to look after their son, my father, and that that person definitely wasn't Rudolph Fentz.

One imagines Ingrid, worried, thinking about what she'll need to bring with her to the hospital, knowing she will not be able to leave the room until she is given the all-clear, discussing things with Fentz in their tiny apartment. The baby, my aunt, who was six years old at the time and not really a baby, is in the next room, crying, probably scared. *Why haven't you given her her dinner yet?* Ingrid asks Fentz. *I've been talking to the doctors all day, going from this office to that one, and where were you? Where? Do you really care so little for this family you can't spare a moment to feed your daughter?* Perhaps this is too much; perhaps, I mean, I am overcorrecting for my father's lack of emotion. Oh well. Ingrid, turning from the counter, brandishes a knife, and Fentz scampers from the kitchen. *Coward!* Ingrid says. She had merely been making a sandwich to bring with her—who knows whether they'll feed her? Only a coward, she thinks, a coward like her husband, would have seen the knife in her hand and the tone in her voice as threats. And anyway, what kind of person would you have to be to think that *she*, Ingrid, a mother so devoted she was putting her life in danger just to be there with her son, would do such a thing, even if she wasn't getting any help at all from her husband? This person who had promised *in sickness and in health* was trying to bury his head in the sand, hoping the whole thing would just go away if only he didn't look at it. Was he *afraid* of their son? Was he afraid of her? She heard what she thought was Fentz rifling through the closet for something—a bag? a coat? nothing was missing from the apartment when later they checked—and then saying, muffled by the closed door, *I'm going to see my son.* This was the last anyone ever saw or heard of Rudolph Fentz.

My son, the boy who, at the end of daycare, used to grab hold of the polka-dotted bolted-down tables and refuse to let go just so he could keep playing with the white-and-blue stuffed bird he had already spent all day with—Zazu, maybe?—wrestling with his aide while his mother or I waited nervously outside for that aide to appear at the door with him, would almost certainly want me to say that this illness my father had was later found to be hereditary, and so the fears of contagion he describes were completely unfounded. My son would, if disappearances were, instead, birds, tell me that 76%—a number I've made up; no doubt my son would know the correct number if missing persons were his passion—that is, a sizable portion of all disappearances are really something more like the resistance he put up at daycare, I mean men and women who, obstinately, do not want to be made to appear, do not, that is, want to be forced to go on with their day, and he would want me to say that, furthermore, the police do not consider a person missing for several days for a very simple reason, because, if those police suspected they had a murder on their hands rather than a missing persons case, those days they insisted must pass before they could begin their missing persons investigation would instead be considered absolutely crucial to the investigation, so crucial, in fact, that those same police would tell you there is only the slimmest of chances of solving such a case, 13%, say—again, my son, no doubt, would have the number on the tip of his tongue if such percentage referred to birds—if no evidence turns up during those first few days, and that the case would then be called *cold*, so that the reason the police don't consider someone missing until several days have passed has at least something to do with the fact that the police know those missing people would really prefer not to be found, and so it's only polite to just leave them be.

But then my son would not tell you any of that, because none of it involves birds and he really only cares for birds. When the sun has gone down and there is barely a glow around us at the edge of the grocery store parking lot—where, it should be said, we'd gone only to get the hot dogs my wife, at home, is waiting for; *Take him*, she'd said, obviously tired, and I'd relented mostly out of guilt—and I try to take the binoculars from my son's hands and he holds on so tight I can see his muscles tense even in the semi-darkness, and I almost feel I can hear the scream I know is coming, and I look around to see just how many people are going to see me smuggle him into the car thinking I'm a pervert, or a bad dad, or who knows, and when I'm sitting behind the wheel, finally, holding the cooling—though now only slightly so, having had time to warm up in the locked car—package of hot dogs to my eye and I've almost but not quite swallowed my frustration and am able to speak in a relatively calm tone, telling him it's all right, my eye will be better in no time, that I love him no matter what, I'll look over and see he has turned on the dome light so he can scan his Audubon, and I'll want to say, *You know, it's also possible Rudolph Fentz went to the hospital but no one remembers seeing him there*, but my son will have no idea what I'm talking about, and so we'll both sit there in the car, staring ahead, him at his book and me at the road.

Given how short my father's letter is, it would seem ridiculous to drag this out any further; I've already written twice as much as he did. So, let me come to the end and tell you about the strangest part of his letter, the part I puzzled over and which, ultimately, set me to writing this. My father, though he often seemed quite taciturn to me growing up, is a feeling person, a man of sensitivities. Maybe it's that he's melted over the years, softened, or that I have. Though he never—not once—brought up the subject, still, he could not but have felt the loss of his own father acutely and for nearly the whole of his life; just the fact of it seems enough to excuse his silence. And yet, despite this, despite what I know or at least must hope is there, somewhere, in his heart, at the end of the letter, just where it would seem excusable, even appropriate, for sentiment finally to creep in, perhaps anger or even self-pity, there are instead two fairly long paragraphs on the subject of conscription. The history of it, I mean, not his feelings on it. I think, given what's there, that it's much too generous to say he was trying to say his father had been drafted or shanghaied, somehow pressed into service, on the way to see his son in the hospital. It's laughably improbable anyway, and there is no such connection drawn in the letter. There are just these two paragraphs on conscription, presented without context, as though my father had forgotten which letter he was writing. Did someone out there have a letter with all the emotion missing from the one I'd received? Some history lesson that suddenly swerved into absence and loss? I think probably it's too much to hope for.

Perhaps, then, to make up for this strange and disturbing absence in my father's letter, I should tell you my own feelings about this thing I am myself now writing, this thing you are reading: It is, of course, imperfect in almost every aspect, as anything is—there are too many abstractions at the beginning, it doesn't get rolling until the second or third page, and so on—but then maybe, I'd like to think, it only seems that way because of my own unreasonable ambitions and expectations for it. I would like to say that it is something of which I feel proud, even if only really in the most thrilling moments of its creation, before I had a chance to look it over and compare it to my fantasies for it, before I'd found it wanting and then slowly, agonizingly slowly, realized it was really only me that was wanting, me that was disappointing. Does the frustration come from the fact that I've finally put into words this suspicion I've had for so long, that whatever there is in me is corrupt, and so whatever comes out of me will be, too? I look over the top of the laptop's screen at my wife trying to hurry our son through his morning rituals so that she can get his sister to daycare and still get to work on time, and then, later, at my phone as I sit in the car, waiting to work up the courage to face my son's aide after yet another fight at school, and I wonder about those long-ago comparisons my father made. How was I like Rudolph Fentz? Was there time to change? Was there really the will to? Perhaps it is better to write about birds, I think, or conscription. Just the facts.

TWELVE

Laurie Stone

I am twelve, and whatever people think they know about girls, they do not know or they are lying. Where I lived there were houses under construction and the clean, splintery smell of jetties. In the house there is a chair and ropes to tie your hands, a blindfold. There is a chair and a boy. At the end of the block the street melts into the dunes, and the dunes are shaped like a body. The boy smells of fresh sweat. There is a glisten in the smell, and a drop hits my shoulder, and when my hands are free I touch it. We are on the second floor, and before us is sky where soon there will be a wall. The workers have all gone home. It's quiet. His collar is open. His hair is thick and sandy. This is not like anything I have imagined would happen when I woke up. There is no touching other than the game. It's his idea. After this, I will look for people with ideas. The boy is not a friend. We have seen each other around. He whispers into my neck, and I am happier than I have ever been. The blindfold is a cotton square, rolled and tied around my head. I can see through it to sky and clouds. He says, "Is this what you like?" I say, "I don't know what I like." I say, "Yes." I am wearing shorts and a polo shirt. My hair is in pigtails. I am not a lovely twelve-year-old, but I have become thin by dieting at camp. I have peeled off the breading on veal cutlets and become thin. This is not a memory. Memories are unreliable. The boy's name is Rick or Ricky, and there are muscles in his freckled arms. He ties my hands with a piece of jump rope or a ribbon from my hair. He is beautiful. I can't tell you how I know this is inside me. I dream about the house when I am awake. I am not his captive. There is a set of swings near the house where we meet to play the game. He pushes me languidly. It's private. I am a girl about to be discarded by her best friend. In another version, my friend and I enter the house, and the boys circle us. We wrestle with them until we lay on our backs, breathing hard. My friend gets a splinter in her finger, and I pull it out and lick the blood. I don't know what my wanting does to the boy. He looks at me the way you watch a butterfly dance with restless legs along a branch. I don't know what my wanting does to my friend. She sits with other girls now at lunch. When I grow up, I will not know if wanting people scares them or if they leave for other reasons.

FIVE POEMS

Iris Cushing

The Third Bacchae

Orange notebook
with orange notes
                              yellow tabby
                                        in peech-tree dusk

                                        A blaze, a

spark in the cuff
                    of a pleather boot

like the white tin speck of a plate
                              enameled blue

a night sky
becomes this plate, a cup

                              Tina and me
                              become
                              two of three
                              bad bitches

clad in silverware skins
around a flaming pit
in a painting

                              Who will be the third Bacchae

If you stop reading this,
you'll die

a home for wasps, a paper comb   up a tree

my poem
                    is notes taken   a whole lotta notes

                        when will I sit
                        and stitch them
                        into a dress

                        for her,

                        Buckskin Barbarella

Claustrophilia

Outside the snow fills this Tuesday with itself, its near ice, faint shapes of things left outside.

Or already outside: things naturally outside of things.

This room is larger than most prison cells, but still you think of prison, of imprisonment.

The inside of inside. This is the only place where good is found, Kant wrote.
A place unknown to the outside world and unfathomably small.

Unfathomable. A body doesn't leave its dwelling for long periods of time.

On days like this, thick winter days, you think of Hannibal Lecter in his stone-walled cell, drawing remembered vistas on thick paper with charcoal. Memory, Agent Starling, is what I have instead of a view.

Claustrophilia. The love of being in a confined space. Kant kept such a strict schedule that his neighbors set their clocks to his routines. There goes Immanuel, it must be three o'clock. Or whatever they called "time" three hundred years ago.

I sat beside my friend who is a monk on the bus from the city to the country. I recalled to him my own wish to be a nun, a teenaged wish. There was a painting I'd loved of a nun in a garden titled *Convent Thoughts*.

"I am a garden monk, that's who I am, I don't wish to be anything else," he told me, gesturing with his thin-skinned hands, smiling through the soft creases of his eyes.

Many are inclined to think of monasticism in terms of what is lost. Sexual intimacy, property, autonomy (*auto*=self; *nomos*=law). For some it is a great gain, an immeasurable gain.

Enter a field that contains the prisoner, and the monk, and the philosopher, and the poet.

Or a night sky: each one being a star, the holder of an intensely bright sovereignty.

At the center of each point is pure will. The points touch each other through the light they give, but they don't meet in real space.

Clarice, always on the other side of the glass.

Fear

Dry leaves move revealing a scent—the place at the foot of a tree
they've protected all season. The soily damp place now exposed,
leaves taken to shelter another patch of soil.

The scent is all around for a moment, warmed by the silent mountain
air and the white noise of water several hundred yards away,
and the bark of a dog in the distance.

The scent is too near to be near to it, the color of an inner substance, a
       substrate.
Sure there are scents of pine and woodpecker, but this scent isn't
       something on a list:
catch up with your correspondence.

Your correspondents. What does the inside of your mind look like to you,
Caitie asked me last week. Dreams about houses with furnished rooms
unoccupied for a fearful length of time.

But inducing something more than fear. The room we were talking in
had high ceilings peeling creamy paint flakes. The sensation of
       something long lost
to be found past the narrow entry into that room, if you are small
       enough to wriggle through.

The scent that rises from the base of a tree in early spring is something to know.

Stevens writes that the rational is to the irrational what the known is to
        the unknown.
John Cale sings that "fear is a man's best friend."

And I want to sing along with him.
To think of my life outdoors as a place to grow grammar.

In this metaphor, the things that grow are the nouns (parsley, scallions,
chamomile, cabbage, onions, sweet peas and beans).

The soil is the verb. And the other elements are the necessary periphery,
the Haloes (tools, light, water, wind, insects, animals, molds, fungi,
temperature, minerals, rituals), the fringes.

Sweet peppers, sweet William.

Jonathan Edwards used the word "sweet" to describe the sensation of
God's grace mixed with God's grandeur. A living knowledge.

Did Edwards fear God, as I fear the wasted dream-rooms left for years
in the habit of stillness? Once I decided my dreams of abandoned rooms
were about my grandparents, who when they died left me a very small
        fortune.

I described this connection to a holy man. "Make your room look the
        way you want
your mind to look," this man said on another occasion. You get close to
knowledge like the kind found in a room in a box of papers and clothing
smelling like someone but

you lose your way. You want to do something else, so you step out at the
        crucial moment.
But the closeness is there. No matter if you find it. It can't be taken back.

Evening coming on a snowy day

Branches bearing snow blown on them hold their load into the light

that draws away a little slower today than yesterday.

The shapes seen from the comfort of home—pillows, cold desserts, cotton—

more distinct as they join the colors of the ground.
It's a white that keeps to itself

as it becomes gray and then vanishes. Gusts come up from the valley

and move snow into the air even as it's almost dark.

This will continue throughout the night.

The shape of a gust seen for an instant against a mixed background:

pine boughs, closer and further surfaces, free verse.

Last night the space around the iris of each eye was so white and flat,

of you, of the private place we share becoming more private.
Narrowing as an aperture narrows and narrows.

We turned more toward each other as the night passed, a union deeper in stages as the days in stages are longer.

The whites of your eyes as they opened and opened to see me.

That dual piece of you that burned the air between us.

The Listeners

The books are frenching

one open, face-up
another open,
face-down on top

(Plato's *Symposium, Collected Shelley*)

By the hiss of a sappy flame
in a small black rock ring
into a plastic phone I told my God

I picked lamb's quarters and purslane

my God replied
"you've gathered
the eighteenth century"

but

It isn't that easy
people don't even use
telephones anymore

it's a fetish,
a destination

By the time
this notebook ends
a wild telephone
will run through this land

Tina makes us trespass ruins:
the granite gazebo shades
a cistern of cold white sulphur water,

                            waters frenching,

fraying the Village of Sharon Springs,

                            Population What.

Mailbox shaped like miniature house.

mailbox and telephone: listeners.

EXCERPTS from *SINGLE MOTHER*

Marina Yuszczuk
translated from Spanish by Alexis Almeida

1

To get pregnant by mistake is one way to get pregnant. And what is
a mistake? Something that wasn't in the plans, which is to say that no
one had imagined it. Something that you regret after it happens, or a
desire so intense you didn't recognize it, and your body went ahead and
fulfilled it.

2

The sleeveless one-piece that had a fish on its belly

against a background of tiny blue stars

the two that Ana brought, striped, that fit so well,

one blue with red stripes, the other white and black

a robe and the morley pants that came in a cloth envelope with a small
hat

four or five tiny cotton hats he never let me put

the grey terrycloth on him, which didn't seem like a big deal but it ended
up looking so nice

the gray one that had a tiny robot printed on it

the white one with a family of rabbits drawn onto the chest

so tight that once, in the desperation of not being able to get it off

I wanted to cut with scissors

the smooth white, and the tiny pants with prints of animals and with feet

the tiny blue sack with buttons that Graciela knit

the tiny wool blanket that the neighbor gifted him and that once was her
son's

the tiny pajamas with buttons on the front, one white with tiny green
horses

the other light blue with a tiny animal embroidered on the front and the
other with blue

stripes, white and gray

and another, and another, so many pajamas, to wash and change very
often

the tiny turquoise crocheted blanket, white and blue that Ana and Eva
knit

square by square, and afterwards they sewed it all together and they
made

a rattle with the same wool, my poet friends

7

We say to babies, like we say to lovers
"I want to remember this day forever"
and you know you're not going to remember, love
contains a black hole
like the fireworks
that we watched at the end of the year, together, our faces lifted toward
the sky and a secret
desperation
filled us
it was also the coldest new year of our lives
we only lasted a few minutes on the street with borrowed jackets
glasses in our hands
we weren't only looking at the light
but also its disappearance
light is screaming
inside Junio
he was sleeping in his one-month-old body
and unlike the sky he didn't scream
and nothing seemed to touch him
although babies cry and it's normal
now for example
the evening comes and he screams
who knows why
or does anyone know?
As for me, I don't like screaming
I think I hold on to the ideal
of living a life where nobody has the desire to scream
A scream means that everything is broken
and it's true
my baby screams and it makes me a little impatient
it's not that I'm angry
maybe it's a little bit of envy.

8

Run run run
my son
at the speed of the wind

and you leave me behind
and you leave me behind

11

Why do girls drift apart from their girlfriends?

We are enamored
go on a trip together and one day
we stop seeing each other

the last time
that we didn't know was going to be the last time
seemed like it was any other time

and no one says anything
not us or them, nor the rest
and we stay friends

best friends don't leave
best friends dissolve
like a gas in the air, without limits

friends dissolve.

13

This has to be
a book "full of objects"
in a year without words
except for ba ba ba
and tata tá

14

If I resolve myself to say
what is happening to me
or not
if I don't resolve myself.

15

Don't breastfeed him so much
don't pick him up
don't share the bed
I don't think it's good for either of you

it's time to send him to kindergarten
it's time for him to have his own room
it's time for him to understand
that's he's already big

it wouldn't be so bad to let him cry
don't give in to him
just let him cry

just leave him
leave him!
leave him!

THREE POEMS

Nagae Yūki
translated from Japanese by Jordan A. Y. Smith

Blue Water

Alternating memories
Pale blue tinted
Time goes fracturing on

(Every last flower, every form, gone extinct.
Pure nostalgia reigns, saturated fragrance
   Drifting through the water surface.)

Morae melt into syllables
Touched off by fragmented recollections

The gist of reddened bygone days plunged down into extremity
Swaying away
Waning toward silence

Incessantly
Born entangled in collapse, one-hundred billion molecules grow warm,
glow,
Gather the waves in their methylene blue

(Phosphorescent cerulean glimmerings.
That would be a dream.
Unseen by anyone, conserved in a lonely purity,
   never drifting away,
      flickering on at the ocean floor)

Eons ago, there was
A glorious prosperity that often lay down
Whispers
Indignation
All of this now below sea level

The circling recurrence
The demolishing persistence
Prepared for the day of its repetition

And the methylene's blue glare. Rolling waves.
Now only the shadows
Remain straight
Running the water surface

(Between the waves, images wavering
    …Helsi, nki…New, York…To, ky o …..
  Wrong. That would be a dream.
  Unseen by anyone, so modest.
  Cities and flowers too, innumerable abundance,
  Someday, surely,
  Will have gone extinct)

Mortar Stratum of Memories

《tanθ+ sinθ》

Collapsed ambiguity heaped year by year and age by age, this mortar
stratum's upper layer with sounds of a drizzle on mineral mud
mingled exhalations thoroughly spit away patrolling the circumference
of lingering love it's spring it's autumn, we say in vindication, sludge
years slush into hot colloidal gel layer on layer, that red ash surface,
time and again sobering into frozen hard foot soles, embedded all
the more in this mortar layer hot, wet mud colloid, tread the mud
begrudgingly trudging away can't go on, thus carp about it, but while
looking back on it the gel of annual mud assimilated into the mortar
stratum mineral mud lingering love recklessly piled layered finally into
ambiguity this surface of mortar stratum

Festival Music and Plasma

≪ S ≫

Mingled with thunder,
The sounds arrive:
Chin-chaka, chin-chaka!
Here they come, here they come!
Leading the *matsuri*
Musical *hayashi* of tanuki raccoon dogs
Plasma-infused rain
In scorched twilight
Obliviously   running

Evening cicada
Its husk kicked to pieces
One foot   one foot
From the mountain peak, trudging off
Paper lantern processional
Swaying
Lanthanoid's
Faint ballet of descent
Traces spirals
Beneath the eaves,
Lends light to names   of the forgotten

Inside the house, the baby cries

Spinning_spinning of the Urabon festival
Paper lamps in rotation, their glow
In a deserted room
Scattered about, so many sugary drops
Flicker through cell membranes
The *hayashi* drums out any nostalgia
Heat from man-woman interminglings
Drip   drop
Entanglings
The wet crimson *torii* gates

Eight, nine layers, passing through them all
To find Inari's undulating shrine

Smashed
Under the beating *taiko*,
They spark,
Wetted breath
Charmed by the skin
The distant
Gaze
Admiring the height of the grasses
Running off

Pursuing
The pulse

It is certain:
Underneath this shrine,
A boundary once ran

From the slack, blurred rents in the   pressed down, pared away border,
Deep roars on the verge of bursting   embroil the flare in vortex
Damp dangling arm reaches out
—*a child,*   *perhaps*

—a woman,   perhaps
Entangled in the sleeve of a stripped off yukata

Sudden straightness.
Harmonica note sails straight,
Runs off

Clamor of the *hayashi*
Clangs,   vanishes

In the wake of the festival,
The sound-chilled forest of the fox god, Inari,
Hazed out light like uranium glass
Through the intervals of night air,

A figure raising high a bronze-red lantern and
Someone carrying acetylene gas lamp
Nod subtly to each other and breeze by

Somewhere, again,
The baby cries out

EXCERPT from *THEIR INEXTRICABLE CONDITION*

Geoffrey Olsen

I seep into your surroundings where you again emerge to me body positioned—you've come into the room, the room clinging to your discomfort, your desertion of calm. I feel it. You fold into a chair across the room just to sit with me. The AC unit set too cold for you and me pulsing out a little cool sphere against the desert (this you and me imagined). You're talking about your walk, about being out in the desert on the trail, how it felt like the desert was folding over you. You weren't frightened immersed in gentle horizon, and gentle hills massed with cacti curling upward to cradle your awareness.

The sphere holding enclosure and security, functioning as something mechanical, though at the same time as the configuration of Mona's stillness or suffering. Mona's manufacturing of it in the factories of her own center. The cool kept us restive on the days I visited.

Not the mode of preservation, silent absence. Object of desert, a certain kind of privacy.

Placed on the land, You fed on a continuous drift. You walked into the crowd, moving with the people, their calves moving in fabric before you, your psychic arrangement of nearness and proclivity. Civil world burning up, unabated sunlight, condition of drift in an end, dried leaves lay across the gray asphalt. Others wearing light fabrics. You could see their sweat. Each current of your narration was with seasonal transition—conditioning your sensation, awareness, confidence. Green piles up. And blue. And writes it.

By the few lights in the parking lot. No cars, the drift in silence. The light of the fast food restaurant nearby and the road, its hastiness, its lack of specificity. Hell. What you oversaw. The oversight of farming some understanding, some removal from the conditions of your work. Unreceptive and loud. Sensing the sick body. The slow parts. The compression. You list your available options and consider how to take care of yourself. I was unable to witness or to prepare a space, an overgrown salience wide as avenues.

I thought of a time in the restaurant. L was there. We were waiting. We talked about the crowded tables of people as bones pressing one person to another, a threshold of flesh, eating the skin off the animals on their plates. It felt funny and cheap to laugh at the obliging skins slipping away with the edges of the shining utensils vibrating, silvery. L was getting up to go to the restroom. Mona near the desert staying in the small condominium unit.

You, again, operating in the space. I've made it abstract. You's insurgent delight flares as You responds to the objects in the room—the worn books, several stalks of wild grass, dried and brown, pinned to the wall. Far from here in this moment is L observing, watching out their window at night before they go to bed the people crossing the intersection not far from the apartment. L on notice. L noticing, and L like the figure of surveillance or under surveillance. Is there delight in this, like the tension held between L and Mona and You and I, a web? There's no need for austerity all the time, letting the heat outside radiate or throb and the cool filtering it out.

L stuck waiting for the bus, lost in headphones. In this realm, snow dictated an outer disorder, a knowledge when and how to move in the cold. It was just a day when I had to press into the drifts, my jeans dampening as I walked to the grocery store. Mona posted a photo from a recent visit. It was taken indoors, in the gray room with round photo frames of ancestors. One or two held silhouettes of faces in profile, the faces just shadow. The shadow is just outside, just skin. Mona gradually giving away the accumulated heirlooms of her family, piece by piece, before arriving in the desert. A spoon. A pie knife.

You had been how I knew L. That year we would lose track of each other for stretches of time. A month or so would pass. Feeling as though you were present, though that sensation accompanied with a persistent notion of being weighed down by your presence. I couldn't situate how many neighborhoods away you were, yet I felt like you were there, and bothering me. Anyway, it was persistent. I can't remember the weather from that time.

An angle general as a caress, you holding me or a tongue like a soft L sound. My anxiety watching a man in the room, standing in black jeans, inscrutable their light red coat. Something thrumming "no" in the blank place of me, an outline I want of myself like a border I drew.

If I asked where you were constrained, what constrained you to You. That way the shadow of You stuck to your angles like an apparel, that I began to address You as yourself as if through a process of memory, an expectation in the stream of daily getting coffee together or meeting on the street or at a reading. Where "you" became a form of address, compassionate and absent, one that I repeated.

Relating to You or Mona or L as motion. You wants me to be moving here like in a dance (I'm so anxious about dancing). You forcing me to commit to being physically present. While I am embarrassed, I comply. Later lying on the floor laughing this is not the essay.

Then L and I, resting in positions on the threshold as if marking some survival clarity, a mode encompassing You and Mona as well where there then became a meaning, a construct, a grouping. I call the group the four, the cell, collective as respiration. What I remember about the desert was not its intensity but the depressing consistency of it. Feeling as I looked over the saguaro cacti growing up and down the rocky hills the consistency of the light on and on. No shade. The sound traveling without interruption through the dry valley. L was conscious of shades of intensity that played around the relationship that I couldn't see.

There was the problem of rent and work. L maneuvering between bliss and doubt with utter grace. I'm sorry to write this to you. I'm not funny so I leave You out. Staying within the elaborate array of lines, waiting for subways and grocery checkouts. I felt like someone needed to be laughing all the time, so that laughing could be a form of breathing. I give it a space, like a series of busted-up apartments with our altars and our plants. There's no boundaries sometimes between the earth and space, so it felt like that vacuum was brought down here with the atmosphere just holding on. Did you have the discipline to see it clearly? Your job was administrator and assistant. You didn't take seriously bureaucracy proliferating its tangle.

My tendrils were out fumbling over the environment. So I believed L alighted on me, and in me that resistant contagion that locked me up, collapsing into situations beyond a type of melancholy. Sitting near L on a rocky surface like it's collaboration or partnership. You then too bringing your own connection, as you immerse me in your way—algal, unfiltered water, the pool at the base of the ravine, a weathered can of Pepsi—in this like it's your condition. A type of melancholy fomenting unexpected blocked out in terror, as dream, as unknowing absence watching my own body fail to rest in the morning at the table. For instance working, driving a rental truck.

Each incident equaling collision's self—or was it cohesion's doubt? Amused by the moon, by political arrangements in place as totalizing world. I told L about the time I held my cracked glasses, thumb just below the crack feeling the minuscule difference in level between the sides of the rupture, and then gradually, unconsciously increased pressure. A snap and the lens gave way and I focused on the tiny edge of pain localized in the thumb. Here was the thumb with the dry skin and the little droplet of blood.

Even memory contracts, or Mona achingly looking into the future like it's a tumble recognizing the diminution brought along with the ghosts of other animals, the risks of catastrophic storms. Her future crumbling away suddenly like watching a dream—drastic awareness, collective doom. Yet the question comes up for her about who has a right to call this an apocalypse they've never experienced.

She lifting her white hand, it passing through layers of time, she presses it into strange information passing data like skin, like the whole circulating system of something familiar. The blood warm around her. Attention doubles: she brings you with her. Each patch of light you're there this moment, this is where you set yourself. Slow, not so cold anymore.

L sits thinking about the hallucination, about the barely perceptible world, about the sense in trees and pavement and bus stops—this feeling collected, connected, a gentle pulse of waves (WiFi) moving through their soft flesh and hard bone. Beyond some novitiate scale. Then waiting at the bus stop it's cold and night, by the gas station. They are on Empire Boulevard: a condition sketched over street names, like the cars, the little blood cells in capillaries marked out over the vast body. Some boulevard—the cars too fast and crowding, a few storefronts, nothing welcoming, but over them all an unexpected sky, a sky so orange and encompassing. Letting their ears filter and focus on the smallest sounds—drawing out birds or the wind from the loud traffic, centering themself through the tones.

Embedded in Mona's bloodstream, in weather. Would she live to experience the final extremes of heat encircling the world with death, overloaded veins of life? To eat of this, to eat of it vile and shimmering over human constructions, something made of the confining and cavernous, so one saw not even the roof of the cave, the roof of the mouth, swallowed and desperate.

Me: Forgetting myself. Mona telling me of decomposition. Not strange in a way.

You: Where were you then?

Me: In the yard. Her house. The yard bordering the desert. We were in these metal chairs with white tubing, the paint peeling away from the metal. You know, the kind with worn plastic strips that support your back. I thought about how all these objects around were wearing down, which seemed to give them life. Mona liked that. She seemed cheerful.

You: I thought similar things, not knowing yet how to deal with, you know, the planet. Where I fade into the virtual.

The witness passes. Each thing witnessed passes. Would it pass with the witness? That to move through the passage was to enclose with painful light blaring. Painful light blaring that made it impossible to remember. I mean a series of actions, systematic, each lining up, each accumulating to the witnessed system. Do I hear the witness's calls? What witnessing? Witnessing some pained site, where did one hold it? Like Mona, held. Held in the organs, like the lymphatic system, in the autoimmune response, in heart palpitations and migraines and localized pain and the general feeling of pain and headache and fatigue. Sharing witness. The protraction of my witness which was pleasure or privilege or absence. A real violent knowing witness protracting or projecting my being. What did you, L, Mona, see or feel? You have that, L has that, Mona has that, and through the heart though my heart. I felt the risk or link flickering over the life I led.

Green winter light.

Don't dazzle. There's no glamour. There's no artifice, no despair.

There's not even silence which I witness, that pouring into me, wind blowing leaves from trees, the mass of people around me at the march, the excitement of lights of the cabdrivers stuck in the crowd but still jubilant, honking car horns. A silence Mona slips into. Arguments. White classrooms. Objects. All the sounds—a machine pumping air into the room.

I suspend that of myself, limbs, on the wooden floor with the others, mostly dancers and artists and writers gathered here to find some collective clarity and solace. The time I'm given suspended with the time of the living world, with the weather moving over the surface, a blood cycle, a turning self, each cellular moment in me adjacent to the sphere to cast a protective spheroid (that's what I am told to do) around oneself, to find the spot for me not porous with anger, the anger pouring in duress, I touch my belly, what if it was a furred belly, what if I was a different mammal, a dog perhaps, a deer, a coyote, a bat?

Then you move—flowing from an inner derived system I held something for you in the room, watching you, making sure you were ok, you're slowly raising and lowering your arms, you turn slowly crossing one foot over the other, you slowly descend and then you extend upward. You stopped and opened your eyes to watch me. I leaned into the room's vacuum, eyes closed. I held my arms behind me. I was like the figurehead on a ship pressing forward into the waves the motion. A languid movement. Then I moved my arms, sweeping downward, the gesture enabling a solitude I did not expect.

Later I sat by myself while the others moved.

Where L (dissonant) waiting in a song and with trees, calm: thinking it erotic, somewhere them with another, not seeing them (this is later). It's dark. L being with an outline and shadow who puts them at ease, listening to the song. L watched a documentary on pianist Cecil Taylor and he speaks of practicing and improvising along with the branches outside his window dancing in the wind. They breathe and they breathe and when they breathe each breath they breathe they are filled with total satisfaction.

Mona reading transcripts, piecing together an event and message. Newell Street. She recomposes the message. Sitting in a chair becoming anxious responding to the world. Her anxiety being about what props her up, her being disgusted by it, a structure. Dreaming later of a sea of rugs on the floor.

L lying in the bed feeling around them the materials of the room, the layers of fibers and plaster and dust. One time watching a spider walk across the dusty bureau, the shadows of plants outlining the spider's passage. L then in the elegance of thinking and watching. Elegant L, them hearing the traffic, the world not suspended but spiraling outward from the point they occupied. A hearing that turned around the obligations and pleasures that called to them in turn.

L getting out of bed, putting on layers of clothes, layering against the cold. Trees wait in the universe.

Would L sing to the plastic bags held in winter tree branches? Retrieved song placed sidewalk cracks, spilt point. All the life in the unseasonable, going forward in the perpetual unseason. A song that dissipates a barrier or in meeting another, a barrier dissipates.

What I saw of time a presence in merrymaking. Winter, some unexpected, not a presence to the devastation. What was that past, Mona, that duration named that wore one down? Collective wearing, wearying. Dusty substance. She runs her hand along the bureau, she has not cleaned the dust sticking to her hand.

L in themself the elongating vertebrae, their flexibility and poise that carried them through an understanding where the hologram—projecting and revealing from multiple angles—saturates a deep opening where they stretch their form, porous with the world. How L touches the space where they convene, the loose black sweatshirt hanging slight off their extending arms.

All of this in Mona's dream of floating slowly in orbit, charting the debris—abandoned fuel pods, dead satellites, various fragments of shattered objects—that moved in gradually decaying orbits. For perhaps 150 years Envisat, the European Space Agency's largest civilian Earth observation satellite, will float dead around the planet before it crashes back toward the atmosphere. Its fragments and dangerous debris will put at risk the orbit. Before, the satellite slowly pulsed, breathing in and out. Mona was in it then, and it felt calm and secure, suspended slowly in the intervals of dark and light, absorbing the observable blue below. And feeling then the floating give way, sinking suddenly toward the earth, too fast. Waking, Mona remembered the fall as a form of music, a sudden tonal descent, sweeping downward. The vertiginous sound rushing the consciousness so the satellite fell away and Mona moved free.

FENTANYL HONEYMOON

Derick Dupre

In the course of the day I am valiant twice. I unhitch myself and latch onto a tune, the whistle and trill of a strong fat nuthatch. Which chute do I choose to the vault within. Which ailment awaits its deadening. I'm numb and I itch and can't scratch for shit. For the next few hours you are my lover, my martyr, and my lunatic wife. I have the feeling of being tremendously okay. Okay spreads over me like a jellied knife across hot bread. Which is the first instance of valiance. I unlatch from the bird song and I have the feeling of twitch and sway, a mind-body hula only vitiated by itch. An anvil drops so slowly it feels no greater than a walnut. I am alive and I am haunted. If I had an appetite I'd have half of something. Chopped veal hash and amberjack. Violet flowering chives. Chitlins fried in china white. If I had an appetite. A large hand of smoke or wind beckons like a golden age cartoon. Though when I see a plate that's been enchivened I have sometimes flown into a rage. Sticks of chive will form an X across my dish and cancel my appetite. So I nosedive into a glass of anisette poured over ice. My seaside hotel business has burned to the ground. Now ease into the noose or ready the seasoned oven. This is my synthetic honeymoon. Is it licit. Pay no mind like you don't pay bills. I'm numb and I inch towards a prayer to the council chairmen. The ravening mayors are on the roadside roasting doves from overseas. A stereo blares the municipal message, WHO EATS DIES SOON, and pumps a vapor through its speakers. They are erasing videos and burning screens in a riotous sooty rodeo. A woman with a pushcart stops to smell a rose of sharon. The amazing and the sublime sound like a scourge. I shut my eyes and I'm numb and I inch towards a prayer for being touched. If I had an appetite.

I answer my hunger with a stone in my pocket. This is the second and last instance of valiance. I place a warm stone in the pocket of my robe. Then another. Three more after that. Soon there's a heft of stones in the pocket of my robe. I feel like I'm sinking but I'm no longer hungry. Another stone. A thermal unit. A shiny stone engulfed in coastal light. The warmth spreads to my belly and I'm no longer hungry but I feel like a drink. Another glass of anisette. I move beyond the hunger I do not own.

Moving on, as through a heartbreak. The brunt of the actuality of moving on. How to calculate the actual vacancy rate to see how much of my heart's space sits unoccupied by things that once lived there. How to use the space, the heart's household clothed in scarlet. How to envision a heart without its twin. The many how-to's involved in moving on. I forget names and needs. I need to know how-to.

I breathe in and smell my skin, the smeary grooves and creases of my face. I consider the heart, anybody's but mine. I think the heart will surrender to my appetite. I think of eating the heart instead of breaking it. I think what if I just eat this thing. If I had an appetite. I think of the phrase eat your heart out and imagine a man going down on his own heart and how, inevitably, he will fail to please it.

I'm numb but I begin to feel a warmth, an excitement, a drumming up of the senses. For a brief moment I am beside myself with memories of sensation. I think about let's talk about feelings. I remember what to touch. It's always been soil. Tilling the land with a clumsy fist. An hourglass that's packed with earth. There is a subterranean quality to what's going on within me. Everything is like a seed from which will bloom true feelings, blooms of my ideal selves like several long takes of nature pastiche, my ideal selves captured at a low frame rate, flowered, culled, rearranged, and placed in water to die a slow and decorous death.

It stops. The feels stop. Prayer has failed me and so's the earth. Goodbye my love, goodbye crude touch. I'm numb and I itch and I don't know how. I'm numb no more than I know how-to. I don't know any more than I ever knew. But I'll never know if I don't know now.

DOTS ON THE HORIZON

Tsipi Keller

But I say it's fine. Honest, I do.
And I'd like to be a bad woman, too,
And wear the brave stockings of night-black lace
And strut down the streets with paint on my face.

—Gwendolyn Brooks

After a climb of three flights she is finally home. The familiar silence a presence all around her, Woman is glad to be home. Alone. She likes the word. She likes the sound of alone, even if its twin echo connotes abnegation. Words gather in and around her; she's a scavenger. Still, she is real to herself and possibly to others. She goes to her place of work and watches her boss pull at his crotch as she sits across his immaculate desk and listens as he drones on about corporate culture and ethics. He mentions a dot on the horizon and she nods, keeping her stare on his face, doing her best to not give away that she's aware of the hand underneath his desk. At times, she watches him and his executive chair catapult through steel and glass and magically vanish from view. At such moments she admits to a hardness inside her, a hardness she is unwilling or unable to break; a hardness that keeps in check the bubbles of rage that do sometimes rise to the surface and burst in explosive flames. One afternoon, during one such eruption, an urge to rewrite her life possessed her. She grabbed her bag, gave her boss the finger, and left.

Woman looks out the window where all is shimmery white and humid and wet. It is a new morning, a summer day in the city. She makes coffee and goes to her desk. A smidgen of apprehension, her collaborator, follows close behind; she must justify her existence. On the screen, Woman does and says things that are foreign to her, or maybe not altogether foreign. At this very instance, she is experiencing a moment of euphoria laced with anxiety. She gulps down a couple of vodkas to be ready for him, the potential man of her dreams.

Silly, silly Woman. A marionette, she pirouettes across the screen where she dwells. She is serving a purpose, but, in the end, it will seem that her life has become so very small, so very insignificant, that it will have to be snuffed out. Like a dot on the horizon, Woman will fade from memory as if she never existed. The police may conduct a short investigation, but soon dismiss the case as yet another female found dead in the park. No one will miss her and, a week after she is buried, no one will speak her name.

Woman feels a sharp pain in her left breast. She puts her hand under her shirt, squeezes the soft flesh. It is not true that cancer doesn't hurt, a friend once told her, and Woman begins to fret. But soon, as if responding to her touch, the pain goes away. Like Woman on the screen, she, too, sometimes says things she doesn't mean. Not an unusual occurrence in polite society, but Woman later broods about it, and becomes ashamed. If there's a constant in her life, it is shame.

We're all beggars with dreams, Woman reflects. It is two o'clock, and she is out on the street. A homeless man sits on the pavement, leaning against a marble column near the entrance to Duane Reade. As Woman approaches, he pitches forward, reaching for her passing feet. Coarsely he whispers: I want pussy. My dick hurts. Woman feels for him, but she can't help him. On University Place, a young girl, sporting a generous cleavage, comes toward her, and Woman sees herself in the girl, some twenty years back, half displaying her body, half hiding behind it: half tacky, half shy, maybe half aware. The girl's delicate breast flesh, hoisted and exposed, quivers with every step, and Woman tries to remember what made her bare her breasts when she was her age. Was it pure delight in her blooming flesh? She remembers one particular summer day, walking down the street in a new bluish-grayish mini dress, acutely and tensely aware of men looking at her a certain way; she felt seductive, self-conscious, and foolish.

Lately, she's become more attuned to her neighbors, is more attentive to doors opening and closing in the hallway. Sometimes, when she thinks she hears an unusual sound, she peers through the peephole, but usually it is just a neighbor taking out the trash. Now she hears Vivian, her next-door neighbor, laughing and talking, her dog howling with the contentment of his mistress and her friends. She's been hearing them all morning, possibly out-of-town guests, coming in and out of Vivian's apartment.

Mildly jealous, Woman is thinking: They're having a full day, coming and going. It is Saturday afternoon. The sun is shining, and an entire weekend, full of activities, is still ahead of them.

And now the couple at the end of the hall is at it again—not a day goes by without the woman screaming, and not a peep out of him. Do they ever sleep, Woman wonders; sometimes she hears them yelling in the early morning. A few days ago, one of the neighbors called the police. One day, Woman is thinking, he will kill the woman, if only to shut her up. They both have long dark hair, and wear narrow dark glasses. They are quite attractive together, and the guy's lean physique and hard-edged cheekbones suggest something of the wolf. He is a musician, and Woman often hears him go at his guitar behind his door—a discord of mournful sounds. He always seems withdrawn, maybe drugged, and hardly returns her greeting. But on Fourth of July she met him in the hallway, and something compelled her to ask, "Are you going to watch the fireworks tonight?" and he said, "I have enough fireworks in my life," which made Woman laugh and instantly like him. Some time ago, on her way to the trash chute, she heard them have sex, and, unable to stop herself, she approached their door to listen. From the way the woman yowled, Woman surmised they were doing it doggy-style. She waited in hope to hear a moan from the musician, but he was as silent as a monk, pushing into the woman, maybe with contempt, maybe with love.

On the floor above, a young guy died of an overdose. He rotted in his apartment for days until the stench brought in the authorities, the clean-up crews. The guy's dog survived, and a rumor circulated in the building that the hungry dog gnawed on his master's corpse. Soon, a new tenant will move in—a fortuitous opportunity for the landlord to jack up the rent by thirty or more percent.

There are no children in the building, only impaired adults living with their pets. And the pets die, too, of disease and heartbreak. Yesterday, getting her mail, Woman saw Ralph, a retired janitor. "Where is your dog?" she asked; she usually sees him with a scrawny, grayish poodle.

Ralph looked at her from behind his tinted glasses. "After my wife died, he died." He sniffled, quivering at the mouth. "I found him the following morning, stiff as a log. If you think animals don't miss their masters, forget it."

She nodded, feeling awful and painfully embarrassed. She did not even know that Ralph had a wife; she never saw her. And so, the wife died. And now the dog. And then Ralph will die. And the building lives on, its decaying walls recycling humans like so much waste.

Her real life, Woman reflects, happens precisely when she is not engaged in life or thinking about it. In the park, leaves begin to turn yellow and fall to the ground. The three old ladies she has come to cherish as *her* old ladies are walking briskly, and the tall one among them, as always, does most of the talking. These three old ladies are different from Woman. These women, it is obvious, have raised families, it was their first priority. Woman and most of her friends are single and childless, having learned early on to preserve and cultivate a youthful look—their first priority?

Grave-looking men and women, carrying briefcases, tote-bags, backpacks, go past her on their way to work. Watching them, Woman is struck by the thought that while they have to rush to work, she, the bum, can loiter in the park. She can stand all morning if she so chooses and watch several grackles take a shower under a dripping faucet. Watching the birds, it is clear that they know the meaning of standing in line and waiting their turn. In recent weeks, she's had a couple of dreams where she is back in the office and seemingly quite happy. Her employers had called and asked her to come back and she did, she went back, working part-time. In the dream, it suddenly hits her that she does not want to be there—why did she ever agree to come back? How is she going to extricate herself? At this point she wakes up, as if from a nightmare.

She sits for a while on a bench, feasting her eyes on the remaining green leaves on the trees and listening to the quiet in her head. She then rises and walks around the oval, rotating her arms. An old lady, coming toward her, laughs and says, "You're terrific," and Woman, seeing in this woman a divine messenger, happily responds, "Thank you!"

Woman is talking to herself in the mirror. The mirror talks back, mirroring, and Woman on the screen, jittery and anxious, is also spinning in mirrors; something, she does not know what, gnaws at her. Rehearsing, she raises her hand and kisses it, all the while observing herself in the mirror and trying to see what she looks like when her head is inclined just so.

Looking in the mirror, Woman thinks of Vivian. Vivian with the high, nearly Mongolian, cheekbones, the glistening coils of thick hair that run loose on her shoulders, the strong, sensuous nostrils, the wide mouth. When Vivian laughs, Woman can see into the velvety depths of her mouth. Some women have this look—hard, and fiercely independent. The look says: Don't mess with me. Woman often wishes she had that look. During one of their short encounters, Woman mentioned Thoreau, and Vivian asked, "Thoreau?" and Woman said, "The writer?" "Oh, yeah," Vivian said vaguely, and Woman felt very stupid.

On the screen, Woman laughs like Vivian, but in the mirror, when Woman tries to laugh like Vivian, she is too embarrassed vis-à-vis herself, and she has to stop.

After breakfast, Woman settles on the couch with Jane Bowles and her *Two Serious Ladies*. Miss Goering is in bad shape. She is having drinks with the big man who keeps insisting, in spite of her protestations, that she is a working prostitute. Not a small-time prostitute, but a medium one. Miss Goering laughs: She had no idea she looked like a prostitute, she says. A derelict perhaps, or an escaped lunatic, but not a prostitute. The man's chauffeur drives them to the man's house, where they are served steaks. From there, they drive to a restaurant where the man has a meeting with three brutal-looking men; Miss Goering is to sit at a table by herself and wait. Bored, she calls Mrs. Copperfield, who, indeed, is back from Panama and is delighted to hear from her friend.

Mrs. Copperfield arrives with Pacifica, who reminds Miss Goering of her own Miss Gamelon, although Pacifica, Miss Goering has to admit, is a much nicer person and physically more attractive. Mrs. Copperfield, Miss Goering notes, is terribly thin and seems to suffer from a flare-up of the skin. She is as high strung as ever, gulping down her double whiskeys, occasionally spilling some on her chin; Mrs. Copperfield confides that she has gone to pieces, something she has wanted to do for years.

Something she has wanted to do for years—Woman marvels. This is something that she, too, has wanted to do for years. Allow herself to go to pieces. An anarchic aggression directed at the self. At times, Woman allows herself to let go, but not for long. And she does not venture too far. She always comes back, has never allowed herself to go all the way to the other side.

At her desk, she writes: "I said to myself today: Who are you little girl? Why are you hiding? Why don't you let your sadness shine? Why must you concern yourself with every little thing? Who put you in charge? Accept your small place in the world. True, you did not bother to build a nest, to be socially active in your community. Live with what you have. And remember: Every plus comes with a minus."

Later: *Quiet. House clean. Sipping coffee after shopping for food. A domestic day. Rearranged and dusted some of the books. Suddenly stenographic style—why? Quiet. Very quiet. And peaceful. Still. Very still. Must think hard to recall such comforting stillness in the heart. Very little traffic. It must be the quiet in me after housework, scrubbing everything clean, and then myself under the shower.*

Dinner baking in oven. Fingers smell of cilantro, and Verdi's Macbeth *nearing its end on "Live from the Met." After dinner, read, and maybe some TV. On the whole, a relaxed domestic day, much accomplished, pleasant chores when not too pressing and frequent, tomorrow work, today, unpredictably, a day off, sort of. It is vital, is it not, to find something to cling to, something that is tangible and intangible at the same time, for what else is there, the buying and the selling, the moving or the staying in the same place, the consuming, the chitchatting.*

Later still: *The words on the tray!—I suddenly remembered as I ate my dinner. The words from a dream dreamt a few nights ago, cautioning: You need more sleep!— too mundane, really, and therefore disappointing, so maybe the words I thought I remembered when I woke had nothing to do with the tray in the dream. Maybe the remembered words were left over from another dream, a generic and often repeated admonition to take better care of myself, but the more I thought about the tray that morning, and the more I tried to recollect the feeling of reward I thought I had felt upon waking, the less glory attained to the tray, as it, too, in its propinquity to food, finally seemed mundane, there was no getting around it, so I rose from the bed and played* Aznavour, *even though I had meant to play* Schubert, *and I cried a little with que* c'est triste le Venice, *telling myself I must not listen to music, not to this kind of music, music that brought back the past, that talked of love, no, I shouldn't listen to this music, I thought, then thought again, telling myself that yes, I should, should let my emotions come to the fore, even if ugly, even if admitting defeat, and yes, it was okay to* s'accrocher l'air pitoyable, *you are not a machine, I reminded myself, even if at times I act like one, as for instance today when I looked for a number in my* CONTACTS *and came across numbers I never call anymore, numbers that never called me anymore, and, like an automaton, I set about systematically erasing the numbers and names, and the emotions that went with them, and possibly even some fond memories, and each name and number I deleted made a swishing sound as it vanished forever from the small screen of my phone, a swishing sound that for some reason made me think of dead insects, like hated mosquitoes, and as I deleted the names I wondered why I even bothered, why not let the names and numbers remain among my* CONTACTS, *I might need them again someday, and even if I never need them again, why be so final, so brutal about the names and my relationship to them, and this ushered in the thought that one needed to live in order to write, even if "to live" meant the small drama involved in deleting people's names and associations, people who were still very much alive; still, it was out of character for someone like me to go about it so calmly: I, who never had the heart to delete from my phone or my phonebook people who had died, now found it so easy to delete the living.*

Late night, on **PBS**, Woman watches the giant male tortoise raise himself onto the female; each slow and laborious thrust is accompanied by a long, hard grunt. Tortoises, she learns with wonder and envy, become sexually active only at age fifty, but have a hundred years more to practice.

She climbs onto the bed and props up the pillows. She feels a little old doing this, maybe lonely, aware as she is of every movement she makes. It is strange that she should feel this way, and yet, it is a moment that invites introspection as she goes through the motions, preparing for sleep. She pulls up the covers and reaches for her book and reads a page or two. Her eyes beg sleep, and Woman struggles to keep them open, reluctant to let go of the day, to place the marker in the book and call it a night.

NOTES ON CONTRIBUTORS

LINDSAY REMEE AHL has work published or forthcoming in *The Georgia Review, Hotel Amerika, Barrow Street, december, BOMB, The Offing, Drunken Boat, Fiction, The Brooklyn Rail,* and elsewhere. She was a Fletcher Fellow at Bread Loaf for her novel *Desire* (Coffee House Press) and holds an MFA from Warren Wilson in Poetry.

ALEXIS ALMEIDA grew up in Chicago. Her recent poems and translations have appeared or are forthcoming in *Prelude, BOMB, The Brooklyn Rail, Quarterly West, Gulf Coast, Dusie, Action Yes,* and elsewhere. She is an assistant editor at *Asymptote* and a contributing editor at *The Elephants.* Her chapbook of poems, *Half-Shine,* is recently out from dancing girl press, and her translation of Florencia Castellano's *Propiedades vigiladas [Monitored Properties]* is recently out from Ugly Duckling Presse. Her translation of Roberta Iannamico's *Tendal [Wreckage]* is forthcoming from Toad Press. She was a Fulbright research fellow to Argentina, where she worked to compile and co-translate an anthology of contemporary Argentine female poets. She currently lives in Providence, RI where she teaches writing.

GABRIEL BLACKWELL is the author of four books, the most recent of which is *Madeleine E.* (Outpost19, 2016). His fiction, "A Field in Winter," appeared in *Vestiges_00: Ex-Stasis.* Other fictions and essays have been published in *Conjunctions, Tin House, Puerto del Sol, DIAGRAM,* and elsewhere. He is the editor of *The Collagist.*

ANDREW CANTRELL is the author of the chapbook *Stratigraphy* (2015). His poems have appeared in many journals and anthologies, including *Anomalous, Posit, Lana Turner,* and *Rust Belt Chicago: An Anthology*. As Local Projects, he has performed at the Logan Center for the Arts and the Museum of Contemporary Art. He holds degrees in literature from Georgia State University and the University of Illinois, where he taught English and writing. Originally from Atlanta, GA, he now lives in Chicago where he organizes educational workers. His chapbook *Phantom Equator* is forthcoming from above/ground press.

ANDREI CODRESCU was born in Sibiu, Transylvania, Romania and emigrated to the United States in 1966. The author of numerous books of poems, novels, and essays, he was a regular commentator on NPR's *All Things Considered* and founded *Exquisite Corpse*: *a Journal of Books and Ideas*. He taught literature and poetry at Johns Hopkins University, the University of Baltimore, and Louisiana State University.

IRIS CUSHING is a poet, editor, CUNY teacher and scholar, and reader of texts both popular and philosophical. She is a founding editor of Argos Books and is the author of the book *Wyoming* (Furniture Press Books). Her poems have appeared in *Fence, Boston Review,* and the Academy of American Poets' Poem-a-Day series; she also writes often about contemporary poetry by women for *Hyperallergic*. Currently, she is working on a dissertation about the radical mystic poets Mary Norbert Korte and Diane di Prima. The relationship between matter and spirit is of primary interest to her, as is the false dichotomy between words and actions. Her work can be found at iriscushing.net.

SUSAN DAITCH is the author of *The Lost Civilization of Suolucidir* (City Lights, 2016), *Paper Conspiracies* (City Lights, 2011), *L.C.* (Dalkey Archive Press, 2002), *Storytown* (Dalkey Archive Press, 1996), and *The Colorist* (Vintage Contemporaries, 1990), among others. She is the recipient of two Vogelstein awards, research grants from NYU and CUNY, and a Fellowship in Fiction from the New York Foundation of the Arts. In 1993, her work was the subject of *The Review of Contemporary Fiction*'s Younger Writers Issue along with David Foster Wallace and William T. Vollmann. She lives in Brooklyn with her son and teaches at Hunter College.

S. C. DELANEY has translated, with AGNÈS POTIER, Tony Duvert's prose collections *Odd Jobs* and *District* (published by Wakefield Press). Their work has appeared in *Gargoyle*, *Hayden's Ferry Review*, *Black Sun Lit*, *Animal Shelter*, *Gigantic*, *Kenyon Review*, *Fiction International*, and elsewhere.

LOU PAM DICK (aka Misha/Gregoire/Mina Pam Dick et al.) is the author of *this is the fugitive* (Essay Press, 2016), *Metaphysical Licks* (BookThug, 2014), and *Delinquent* (Futurepoem, 2009). With Oana Avasilichioaei, she is the co-translator of Suzanne Leblanc's *The Thought House of Philippa* (BookThug, 2015). Her writing has appeared in *BOMB*, *Fence*, *The Brooklyn Rail*, and elsewhere, as well as in the anthology *Troubling the Line: Trans and Genderqueer Poetry and Poetics* (ed. TC Tolbert and Tim Trace Peterson, Nightboat Books, 2013). Also a visual artist and deinstitutionalized philosopher, she lives in New York City.

TED DODSON is the author of *At the National Monument / Always Today* (Pioneer Works, 2016) and *Pop! in Spring* (Diez, 2013). He works for *BOMB*, is the books editor for Futurepoem, and is a former editor of *The Poetry Project Newsletter*. Select publication can be found or is forthcoming in *BOMB*, *Hyperallergic*, *The Brooklyn Rail*, *6x6*, *Stonecutter*, *Prelude*, *Fanzine*, *The Atlas Review*, and *LIT*.

DERICK DUPRE is the author of the chapbook *Frail Shrines*. His work has appeared in publications including *Hobart*, *Eyeshot*, *New York Tyrant*, *Sleepingfish*, and *Black Sun Lit*. He lives in Bisbee, AZ.

ADAM GREENBERG's poems and translations have recently appeared in *Asymptote*, *Poor Claudia*, *The Columbia Review*, and *Anomaly*, among others. He holds an MFA in Poetry from Brown University and currently teaches writing at the New England Conservatory.

TSIPI KELLER was born in Prague, raised in Israel, studied in Paris, and now lives in the U.S. A novelist, translator, and the author of eleven books, she is the recipient of several literary awards, including National Endowment for the Arts Translation fellowships, New York Foundation for the Arts Fiction grants, and an Armand G. Erpf award from Columbia University. Her translations of Hebrew literature have appeared in literary journals and anthologies in the U.S. and Europe, as well as in *The Posen Library of Jewish Culture and Civilization* (Yale University Press, 2012). Her latest translation collection, *Futureman*, a volume of selected poems by Hebrew poet David Avidan, was published by Phoneme Media in 2017. Her novel *Nadja on Nadja* will be published by Underground Voices in 2018.

JONATHAN LARSON is a writer and translator living in Brooklyn. Recent work has appeared or is forthcoming in *The Brooklyn Rail*, *Lana Turner*, *Manuskripte*, and *The Volta*. The Song Cave will be publishing his translations of both Francis Ponge's *Nioque of the Early-Spring* and Friederike Mayröcker's *Scardanelli*.

TONY MANCUS is the author the chapbooks *Bye Sea* (Tree Light Books), *City Country* (Seattle Review), and *Apologies* (Reality Beach). He serves as chapbook editor for Barrelhouse and lives outside of Denver, CO with his wife Shannon.

ADAM MCOMBER is the author of *The White Forest* (Touchstone, 2012) and *This New & Poisonous Air* (BOA Editions, 2011). His new collection of stories, *My House Gathers Desires*, was published by BOA Editions in September 2017.

GREG MULCAHY is the author of *Out of Work* (Alfred A. Knopf/Dzanc Books), *Constellation* (Avisson Press), *Carbine* (University of Massachusetts Press), and *O'Hearn* (FC2). He lives in Minnesota.

VI KHI NAO was born in Long Khanh, Vietnam. She is the author, most recently, of the story collection *A Brief Alphabet of Torture*, which won FC2's Ronald Sukenick Innovative Fiction Prize in 2016, the novel *Fish in Exile* (Coffee House Press, 2016), and the poetry collection *The Old Philosopher*, which won the Nightboat Books Prize for Poetry in 2014. She holds an MFA in Fiction from Brown University, where she received the John Hawkes and Feldman Prizes in fiction and the Kim Ann Arstark Memorial Award in poetry.

REBECCA NORTON received her BFA from the University of Louisville in 2004 and her MFA from Art Center College of Design in 2010. Norton's studio practice encompasses 2D and 3D design, collaboration, digital modeling, and animation. Her work explores theories of synthesis and connectivity as they relate to the activity of reconstructing reality in vision and thought. She takes a special interest in the formal mapping of mathematical and generative forms, color theory, the study of perspective in art and architecture, and theories of attraction. Norton has exhibited nationally and internationally, including shows at California State University, Long Beach, CA, The Carnegie Center for Art and History, New Albany, IN, and Schneiderel.Home.Studio.Gallery, Vienna, Austria. She has been a contributing writer for *The Brooklyn Rail*, *Arts in Bushwick*, and *Abstract Critical*. She currently lives and works in Louisville, KY.

GEOFFREY OLSEN is a poet living in Bedford-Stuyvesant, Brooklyn. He is the author of two chapbooks, *End Notebook* and *Not of Distends * Address Panicked*. With writers Lyric Hunter and Sade LaNay, he collaboratively wrote and performed the piece *Tect Heart* at the Brooklyn Arts Exchange in spring 2017. He is a recent graduate of the Pratt Institute MFA in Writing program.

DANIEL OWEN is a writer and member of the Ugly Duckling Presse editorial collective. He is the author of *Toot Sweet* (United Artists Books) and the chapbook *Authentic Other Landscape* (Diez). His writing has appeared in *Hyperallergic*, *Elderly*, *Lana Turner*, *A Perimeter*, *The Brooklyn Rail*, and elsewhere.

ALEXIS POPE is the author of two forthcoming poetry collections, *That Which Comes After* (Big Lucks Books) and the chapbook *Debt* (Madhouse Press). Her work has appeared in *Denver Quarterly*, *Hobart*, *Poor Claudia*, *Powder Keg*, *Prelude*, *The Volta*, and *West Branch*, among other journals. She lives in Chicago.

DANIEL POPPICK is the author of *The Police* (Omnidawn, 2017). His poems appear in the *New Republic*, *BOMB*, *Granta*, *Hyperallergic*, *Web Conjunctions*, *Bennington Review*, and elsewhere. He currently lives in Brooklyn, where he co-edits the Catenary Press.

VICTOR SEGALEN (1878–1919) was born in Brest, Brittany. A French naval doctor, explorer, and writer, he is the author of *Stèles*, a collection of prose poems, and the novels *Les Immémoriaux*, *René Leys*, *Peintures*, and *Equipée*. Segalen was found dead in a forest near Huelgoat with a copy of Shakespeare's works open to *Hamlet* at his side.

STEVEN SEIDENBERG is the author of *Situ* (Black Sun Lit, 2018), *Null Set* (Spooky Actions Books, 2015), *Itch* (Raw Art Press, 2014), and numerous chapbooks of verse and aphorism. His collection of photographs, *Pipevalve: Berlin*, was released by Lodima Press in 2017, and another photo collection, *Kanazawa Void*, is forthcoming from Daylight Books in 2018. He has had solo shows of his visual work in various galleries in the U.S., Asia, and Europe. He is co-editor of the literary journal *pallaksch.pallaksch.* (Instance Press) and curates the False Starts reading series at The Lab in San Francisco.

KYRA SIMONE is a writer and editor based in Brooklyn. Her work has appeared in *The Atlas Review, Conjunctions, Black Clock, The Brooklyn Rail, Little Star, Prelude, Her Royal Majesty*, and *The Wrong Quarterly*, among other journals. She is a member of the editorial collective at Ugly Duckling Presse.

ERIN SLAUGHTER holds an MFA in Creative Writing from Western Kentucky University. She has been a finalist for *Glimmer Train*'s Very Short Fiction Contest, and was nominated for a Best of the Net Award and a Pushcart Prize. Her writing has appeared in *River Teeth, Bellingham Review, Sundog Lit, Tishman Review*, and elsewhere. She is the author of two poetry chapbooks, *Elegy for the Body* (Slash Pine Press, 2017) and *GIRLFIRE* (dancing girl press, 2018), and is editor and co-founder of *The Hunger*. She lives and teaches writing in Nashville.

JORDAN A. Y. SMITH writes poetry and has translated works by Yoshimasu Gōzō (*Alice Iris Red Horse*), Mizuta Noriko (*The Road Home; Sea of Blue Algae*), Saihate Tahi, Kanie Naha, Fuzuki Yumi, and others. Currently Associate Professor at Josai International University, he has taught at CSU Long Beach, UCLA, Roger Williams University, and Korea University. He earned his PhD in Comparative Literature at UCLA and researches in translation studies, Japanese literature, and global comedy.

LAURIE STONE is the author of *My Life as an Animal* (TriQuarterly Books/Northwestern University Press), the novel *Starting with Serge* (Doubleday), and the essay collection *Laughing in the Dark* (Ecco). Her fiction and nonfiction have appeared in *Evergreen Review, Fence, Open City, Anderbo, NANO Fiction, The Threepenny Review, The Collagist, Creative Nonfiction, Memorious, Black Sun Lit*, and many other journals.

MICHEL VACHEY (1939–1987) was a French author of experimental fiction and poetry. He was a founder of the Textruction movement, which sought to blur the line between image and text, and in his writing, visual art informs his style and themes. His work includes novels, collages, and hybrid story-essays.

NAGAE YŪKI's (永方佑樹) first collection, *Lonesome Flowers* (*Monosabishi-no hana*) received the 2012 Poetry and Thought Newcomer's Award (*Shi to Shisō Shinjin Shō*). Her most recent collection, *√3* (2016), employs the language of trigonometry along with images from geology, chemistry, and machinery. She began writing while studying abroad in France, inspired by Sei Shōnagon's *The Pillow Book*, then returned to Japan to study Japanese literature at Keio University. She frequently performs her poetry with video art, dance, and bilingual reading of the translations, including most recently at the Lahti Poetry Marathon in Finland.

MARINA YUSZCZUK is a poet who received her PhD in Literature. She works as a journalist and a film critic for the cultural supplement *Las12 of Página 12* and the magazine *La Agenda*. She has published various books of poetry, including *Lo que la gente hace* (Blatt & Ríos, 2012), *Madre soltera* (Mansalva, 2013), and *La ola de frío polar* (Gog y Magog, 2015). With the press Rosa Iceberg, which she founded with Tamara Tenenbaum and Emilia Erbetta, she recently published *Los arreglos* (2017), her first book of prose. Her first novel, *La inocencia*, was recently published by Iván Rosado.

FORCHCOMING

Situ by Steven Seidenberg
March 13, 2018

To engage with the narrative flow of Steven Seidenberg's *Situ* is to pass through the looking glass of consciousness into a seriocomic world of "mnemonic throes" and "the null of place." I think, therefore where am I? And what? And when? We feel the phenomenal world slip-sliding away, even as we marvel at the charged field of language and thought thus brought to light.

—Michael Palmer

Sheep Machine by Vi Khi Nao
Summer 2018

Vi Khi Nao's poetic ekphrasis of Leslie Thornton's "Sheep Machine" is a visceral companion to an optical theatre of ordinary and extraordinary images that rub off the burning edge of perception.

—Dong Li

BLACK SUN LIT
blacksunlit.com/catalog

AVAILABLE NOW

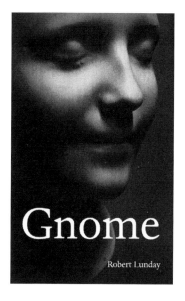

Gnome by Robert Lunday

Gnome—in which poetry takes upon itself again its ancient impulse to think within the beauty it pursues—is worth pondering in all its homonymic oddity. Lunday's book is the guide we did not know we needed: guidebook to our own face, the fact of having a face, all it forms and all that forms through it, expression of eye and expression of words, and those worlds of thought behind the blank stare.

—Dan Beachy-Quick

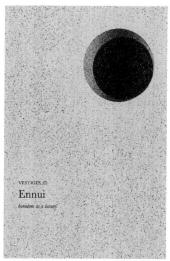

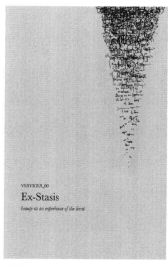

Vestiges_02: Ennui

Friederike Mayröcker, Pierre Senges, Patty Yumi Cottrell, Eugene Lim, Ennio Flaiano, Evan Lavender-Smith, Adam McOmber +more

Vestiges_00:Ex-Stasis

Stéphane Mallarmé, Andrei Platonov, Róbert Gál, Mauro Javier Cardenas, Evelyn Hampton, Gabriel Blackwell, George Szirtes, Elizabeth Mikesch +more